A DIVIDED CHURCH

An Account of the Division in the
Free Church of Scotland in 2000

A DIVIDED CHURCH

An Account of the Division in the
Free Church of Scotland in 2000

John W Keddie

Foreword by William Macleod

**Scottish Reformed
Heritage Publications**

First Published March, 2018

ISBN: 978-1-326-79213-8

Publisher:
Scottish Reformed Heritage Publications
19 Newton Park
Kirkhill
Inverness-shire
IV5 7QB

Printed and bound by Lulu (www.lulu.com).

CONTENTS

FOREWORD

The events leading up to the Division of the Free Church of Scotland on January 20th, 2000 were very unpleasant. I remember at the time when I began my ministry reflecting on a dispute in one of our congregations due to a disciplinary matter which had occurred some years before. It was obvious that the trouble had left deep scars on both the minister and his congregation. My thought was that I must try, at all costs, to avoid something like this happening to me. In my twenty years of ministerial experience up to the point of controversy there were various difficulties at times and considerable patience and humility had to be exercised to keep the peace. I was thankful for the peace I enjoyed and the encouragements in the work.

However, the troubles of the latter half of the 1990s were of such a nature as that they required a stand to be taken. There was no escape if one was to remain faithful to the Lord. Jude states, "Beloved, when I gave all diligence to write unto you of the common salvation, it was needful for me to write unto you, and exhort you that ye should earnestly contend for the faith which was once delivered unto the saints" (Jude 3). From time to time we face a situation when we must earnestly contend for the faith or stand guilty before God as compromisers and those who condone sin. Yet one must admit that it was extremely painful at the time and that, to some extent, the pain remains. It led to division in my own congregation as well as that of others.

I have been asked whether I regretted the stand I made and the actions in which I was involved. Looking back, with the wisdom of hindsight, would I follow the same course again? Without a shadow of a doubt I would. True there were times when I and others could have shown more humility along with firmness, when more gracious words could have been used, but wrongs had to be opposed.

At the end of the day what matters is not what people think of us, our success or our popularity but rather doing what is right in the eyes of the Lord, despite the cost. Soon we will all have to stand before the Judgment Seat. The things that are important to many people today will mean little then. Our concern must be to hear the Lord say to us: "Well done, good and faithful servant" (Matthew 25:23).

In the present work the Rev. John Keddie outlines well the story of the Division of 2000. He enters into no unnecessary detail. He expresses himself always with the gracious courtesy and generosity, which is so characteristic of him. I strongly commend this helpful survey of the issues which led to the division in the Free Church of Scotland. It is a story which needs to be told for the sake of posterity.

WILLIAM MACLEOD
Glasgow
February, 2018

INTRODUCTION

The Free Church of Scotland, a conservative Presbyterian denomination, arose from a 'disruption' within the established Church of Scotland in 1843. This involved the removal of some 480 ministers and missionaries, and hundreds of thousands of people, to form the Free Church of Scotland. The catalyst in this Disruption was 'patronage,' the rights of landowners and heritors to select ministers for congregations. In the early years after the Disruption the Free Church was strongly evangelical in doctrine and practice. By 1900 it had moved from its original positions and entered a union with another Scottish Presbyterian denomination, the United Presbyterian Church, to form the United Free Church. However, a small group of ministers, mainly from highland and island areas of the country, remained out of that union. They appealed through the law-courts to be considered the continuing Free Church of Scotland. In the event they won an historic case in the House of Lords in 1903-4 and so became the heir to churches, manses and funds of the Free Church, though these were subsequently shared with the majority on a more or less equitable basis.

Life was never going to be easy for a Church which was such a small 'rump' of what had been a major Presbyterian denomination in 19th century Scotland. Not only did it not command a significant numerical strength, it was also largely confined to the relatively depopulated highlands and islands for its support. In addition to this it maintained a high view of Scripture as the inspired and inerrant revelation from God, and the theology known as Calvinism. It held to principles of worship in which only inspired materials of praise were used in its services, unaccompanied. These principles were held unashamedly (at least for the greater part). They had become, and remained in general throughout the century, unpopular positions.

It is a mistake to think that such theology and worship were simply idiosyncratic features of highland and island religion. Rather they were principles widely held by Presbyterian and Reformed Churches from the Reformation period, through the Puritan era and into the Victorian age. They were the doctrine and worship which had been characteristic of mainline Churches in Scotland and elsewhere. Rather than being pilloried, the post-1900 Free Church ought to have been lauded for seeking to maintain a regulative principle in Church life that was concerned to remain as close as possible to Biblical teaching. There is also the question of integrity and honesty in relation to *ordination vows*. The post-1900 Free Church unashamedly took a stand for faithfulness in attachment to the Reformed Confession represented by "the whole doctrine" contained in the *Westminster Confession of Faith*.

This did not mean that after 1900 there was not pressure on the continuing Free Church to change and to 'broaden' its theology and worship. There were various trials, but none more so than events towards the end of the 20th century which were to result in the division of the church in the last year of the millennium. In the beginning of 2000 the Free Church divided, resulting in the emergence of the Free Church of Scotland (Continuing) claiming to remain completely faithful to the principles of the Disruption Church and the post-1900 Free Church.

The story of 'aspects of the history of the Free Church of Scotland in the 20th century' has been told by the author in his *Preserving a Reformed Heritage* (first published in 2017). The present work is by way of a sequel to that volume. It incorporates the various factors that were involved in the division in the Free Church of Scotland in January 2000. That division has not yet been healed and has left a legacy of two claimant 'Free Churches' in the 21st century both asserting a Reformed Heritage. However, by an Act of Assembly in November 2010 the larger of the two bodies in the division agreed to permit the use of uninspired materials of praise and instrumental music in public worship. It thus departed from the position of the Free Church of 1843 and

1910. This radical change has made a coming together of the divided church all the more unlikely, as the Free Church of Scotland (Continuing) has continued to maintain the historic position on worship of the post-1900 continuing Free Church.

In examining the division in the Free Church of Scotland inevitably evaluation has been required of perceived flaws in the various decisions and procedures in Church and Civil courts which, it is argued, contributed to that division of 2000. The story is told from the position of the Free Church of Scotland (Continuing) of which the writer is a minister. He became a member in the Free Church in 1968 and an ordained minister in 1987.

The question may be raised as to why these events have been brought up again. Could this sad history not be left in the past? Isn't it unnecessary to recall or dwell on such sad events? These are fair questions. Yet an explanation is required of the continuing existence of the minority section in the division of 2000, now known as a separate denomination called the Free Church of Scotland (Continuing). The very existence of this denomination will be clarified by an understanding of the events leading to its emergence.

It will be noted that this is not an official history of the division of 2000. It comprises the author's own assessment of events in which to a greater or lesser extent he was personally involved at the time. It is understood that a more detailed examination of the issues raised in this book has been commissioned by the Free Church of Scotland (Continuing). Thanks are expressed to the Rev. William Macleod for his kind Foreword. Mr Macleod was Editor of the *Free Church Foundations* magazine in the last few years of the 20th century and more recently the *Free Church Witness*, the monthly magazine of the Free Church of Scotland (Continuing).

JOHN W KEDDIE
Kirkhill, Inverness
March, 2018

UNREST IN THE FREE CHURCH
1990-1995

After 1900 the continuing Free Church of Scotland enjoyed an unbroken history up to the final year of the century. However, an issue arose in the late 80s and early 90s that was to create widespread unrest in the Church. The specific issue that initially triggered unrest was a moral one. The controversy that arose, involving as it did a prominent minister of the Church, clearly had the potential to be a polarising factor in the life of the Church. That it eventually led to division in the Church, however, related to formal action taken in due time through General Assemblies and its Commissions to discipline those who continued to be unhappy about the way the initial matter was handled in the Church. It was all very tragic, affecting as it did the largest of the constitutional, Confessional Presbyterian Churches in Scotland. It is a sad, discomforting story, the story of the rending in two of the Free Church of Scotland in January 2000. The present account of this sad story is told from the point of view of the ministers and people who subsequently came to form what became widely known as the Free Church of Scotland (Continuing).[1]

Allegations of misconduct against a Professor
The issue that initially triggered controversy within the Church centred on allegations of conduct unbecoming a minister of the gospel on the part of a Professor at the Free Church College. As this involved a theological Professor, precognition[2] of the matter was undertaken by

---

[1] This name was adopted solely for administrative reasons by those who, in their view, continued the Commission of Assembly of the Free Church in the Magdalen Chapel, Grassmarket, Edinburgh, on 20th January 2000, upon refusing to accept the legitimacy of the actions to discipline them taken by majority decision earlier that day in the Assembly Hall. This will be explained in detail below.

[2] *Precognition* is the process by which an ecclesiastical court assesses the issues involved

the Training of the Ministry and Admissions Committee in the first instance. The Free Church of Scotland *Form of Process*[3] states that the success of the gospel depends on the blamelessness of the ministry. It reflects the biblical view when it states: "The credit and success of the gospel (in the way of an ordinary mean) much depending on the entire credit and reputation of ministers, their sound doctrine, and holy conversation, no stain thereof ought lightly to be received, nor when it comes before a judicature ought it to be negligently inquired into, or when found evident, ought it to be slightly censured."[4] The principles set out in the *Form* lie at the heart of what eventually led to the sad division of the Free Church of Scotland in the year 2000.

In Church practice the Training of the Ministry Committee in the first instance is charged with processing any such matters involving a College Professor through the Church courts. The allegations in question, involving sexually inappropriate actions, first came before the Committee in 1989, one in the form, initially, of an oral report of an allegation from a woman in England and another in the form of an allegation involving a woman in Australia. However, the Committee at that time never did ask the woman making the allegation in the U.K. to appear before it.[5] In addition, the Committee, on its own admission, failed to obtain a statement from the principal witness in Australia or

---

and the case to be made in a complaint or potentially disciplinary matter against an individual minister. As stated in *The Practice of the Free Church of Scotland in Her Several Courts* (Edinburgh, [8]1995): "in all cases which may lead to a Libel, a careful preliminary examination of proposed witnesses is requisite by the party prosecuting in order that a charge incapable of proof may not be proceeded with" (page 107).

[3] *Form of Process* was adopted by the Church of Scotland in 1707 to provide procedures for the exercise of discipline within the Church. The full title of the Act was: 'Act Approving a Form of Process in the Judicatories of the Church with Relation to Scandals and Censures' (Session 11, April 18, 1707). This *Form* remained the basis for Church discipline after the Disruption of 1843 and continued to be the form used by the continuing Free Church after 1900. The detail of this Act is to be found in Appendix IV of *The Practice of the Free Church of Scotland in Her Several Courts*, Edinburgh, [8]1995, 180-205.

[4] *The Practice of the Free Church of Scotland in Her Several Courts*, Edinburgh, [8]1995, 191.

[5] It may be noted that in this case the Training of the Ministry Committee did receive written responses to questions it asked from this woman in 1993.

from her Church concerning her part in the matter, and no attempt was made to examine another witness who had claimed to have seen an allegedly intimate letter from the Professor to her sister (i.e. the 'principal witness'). A Report by the Training of the Ministry Committee issued late in 1990 made the telling concession that:

> Prior to July 1989 the matter was handled by the previous Convener with the assistance of the Assembly Clerk and Professor [Douglas] MacMillan. This meant that before the Committee launched its enquiry Professor Macleod had already been subjected to questioning and probing and a considerable volume of letters ensued between Scotland and Australia. It is perhaps easy to criticise with hindsight but it is undeniable that the Practice of the Church intended that such matters be dealt with by the Committee and the attempt to steer it clear of the Committee was fatefully flawed and completely misguided.[6]

It should be noted that the Committee in its Report to the 1991 General Assembly did not refer to the fact that it had investigated serious allegations against the said Professor. The matter of such allegations or investigations were neither alluded to nor discussed in that Assembly.

It is to be recognised that this was a matter the members of the Committee had not faced before. The Professor in question was considered to be such an able and highly regarded theologian greatly respected in the Church and beyond. The Committee realised that great care needed to be exercised in the matter.[7] At the beginning of 1993 another complaint involving a woman from Scotland was submitted to the Committee, along with the previous complaint now in written form from the woman in England. As a result of all this, the General Assembly in May 1993 appointed five 'special assessors' to assist the Committee with reference to the particular issues in question.[8] The men

---

[6] *Report on Enquiry by Training of the Ministry Committee into Allegations of Immorality Against Professor Donald Macleod Free Church College*, 13 December 1990. It appears that a communication had been received by the then Convenor who, instead of placing it before the Committee, dealt with it as a private individual.

[7] The author was a member of that Committee, 1993-1996.

would be involved at every point in discussions on the issue. They
would, however, have no formal votes in that connection. As it turned
out, this would be a key matter in the discussion and decision in the
allegations against the Professor.

A sub-Committee, including four of the special assessors, was
appointed to consider the complaints with a view to recommending to
the main Committee whether or not a libel was justified and
appropriate, and what possible form it would take. There is no 'case'
until a libel is raised in a matter of discipline. A 'libel' in Church law is a
formal charge in a particular matter. This presupposes that the question
at issue is not unfounded or trivial, but that there is a case to answer. It
may involve doctrinal deviation (heresy), or a moral fault. Either way it
does not *prejudge* guilt or innocence, but initiates a 'case' by which either
guilt or innocence will be established judicially in the Church. It will be
raised, however, on the basis that a case, as it would become (in the
view of a Church court), is *provable*. In the case of a Professor it is the
Training of the Ministry and Admissions Committee that does the work
in establishing whether there is a case to answer. From there it would
be pursued for action through the Presbytery of which the Professor
was a member.[9] In this case the sub-Committee *unanimously* supported a
Report to the main Committee in which it was recommended that the
matter justified raising a libel in the Church on the allegations against
the Professor.

In the subsequent meeting of the full Committee one member
maintained that the matter of the allegations would not likely be
provable. This influenced even some of the sub-Committee to change

---

[8] *Principal Acts of the General Assembly of the Free Church of Scotland*, Act anent Appointment
of Special Assessors to the Training of the Ministry Committee (No. 25 of Class II)
Edinburgh, 21st May 1993. Strangely, although the *title* of the Act refers to 'Special
Assessors', the *terms* of the Act refer to them as 'special advisers' and 'additional
members.' No mention is made as to whether or not they would have a vote, though in
the end no votes were allowed to them. Although five men were appointed only four
took part actively in the matter in question.
[9] In the Free Church post-1900 this would invariably be the Edinburgh or Edinburgh
and Perth Presbytery.

their mind. On a vote being taken in the full Committee, some of the sub-Committee did not support the Report, and by seven votes to six the sub-Committee's recommendations were rejected. On being asked for their opinion, however, the three special assessors who were present at that Committee meeting (December 1993) all stated and had recorded their continuing support for the sub-Committee's recommendation that there should be a libel raised in this case. The fourth assessor who had taken part in the discussions had sent a letter in to the Committee to indicate a change of mind on the matter. This meant that in that crucial vote of those who reviewed the whole matter present that day, nine were for proceeding to libel and seven (or eight) were against.[10] Such factors as this simply served to complicate matters in assessing the positions of those who were directly concerned with the unfolding of the whole issue within the Church.

The matter comes to the 1994 Assembly (May 1994)

Two Reports came to the General Assembly of 1994. One, the Supplementary Report of the Training of the Ministry Committee simply stated that the matter of the allegations against the Professor had been investigated and concluded that it did not lend itself to demonstrable proof. The other Report was a Minority Report in which it was maintained that the matter was so serious for the Church that, before it was concluded, the advice of the Church's Law Agent and the Principal Clerk of Assembly should be obtained lest the Church open itself up to external action and criticism through mishandling or misjudging a sensitive matter, especially in relation to the women involved.[11]

---

[10] Of the six who supported the sub-Committee's recommendation there were three dissents recorded: Rev Hugh M Cartwright, Rev Gordon Mair, and the Rev John W Keddie. A *dissent* is "a formal entering in the Records of a Court, of a Judge's differing of opinion from the majority, to prevent responsibility, or to exonerate the conscience" (Robert Forbes, *Digest of Rules and Procedure in the Inferior Courts of the Free Church of Scotland*, Edinburgh, 41886, 205).

[11] The *Minority Report* was formally moved by the present writer and was seconded by Professor Hugh Cartwright.

The irony here was that more of the Committee in the end supported the 'minority' report than the Supplementary Report! On a vote being taken in the Assembly the deliverances of the Minority Report were adopted, over against those of the Supplementary Report of the main Committee. The decision of December 1993, therefore, was recalled and the Law Agents and the Principal Clerk were to be asked for specific advice. In the event, the Minority Report kept the matter alive.

Further allegations arise (October 1994)

Whilst the Training of the Ministry Committee met in its regular June meeting it was faced with agreeing a communication to the Church's Law Agent to give an opinion as to whether the Report warranted judicial investigation (i.e. through a Case in the Church courts). A reply came back from the Law Agents and the Principal Clerk by the time of the regular Committee Meetings in October. The Law Agent's advice suggested that the Report did not warrant judicial investigation because of insufficient admissible evidence to prove the serious substance or 'gravamen'[12] "of sufficient of facts or charges to support the major premise or libel." He did, however, advise that if *de recenti* statements[13] were obtained in relation to the two written complaints brought before the Committee in 1993 that would lend some support to the credibility of the allegations.

This, however, was all rather overtaken by events through three further allegations of a sexually improper nature from three different ladies, which allegations came before the Committee at its meeting on 4th October (1994). It was decided that the advice of the Principal Clerk (Rev Professor John L. Mackay) should be sought on these additional complaints. His advice, given the following day, was that such steps should be taken by the Committee to mature the matter by 26th

---

[12] *Gravamen* is a legal term meaning 'the essence or most serious part of a complaint or accusation.'

[13] On *de recenti* statements see note 3 on page 28 below.

October. This meant that the 3 new allegations were expected to be disposed of satisfactorily in just 3 weeks, hardly a realistic time-frame in the circumstances.

The following week a sub-Committee met with the women. An invitation to the Professor to appear before the sub-Committee was, however, declined by him. In connection with the complaints it was felt by at least some on the Committee that an important aspect supportive of the *credibility* of the complainants lay in whether or not they had spoken to anyone else about the alleged incident.[14] Two of the women were able to provide names of those to whom they had spoken about the incidents, as were two of the earlier complainants. However, before such statements were to hand, on 19th October one of the Committee members[15] submitted a paper in which he questioned the credibility of the complainants. In this paper, he suggested that there was 'an orchestrated campaign' against the Professor. In view of the fact that supportive statements were not *at that point* to hand (and later clearly given no weight) this seemed premature and indeed seriously prejudicial. It is more than interesting that one member of the Committee[16] stated that this was a classic response to allegations of sexual impropriety, in that (1) there was the denial of the possibility of the offence; (2) there was the denigration of those making the allegations; and (3) there was the formulation of a 'conspiracy theory.' Notwithstanding this, the paper subsequently became the substance of a *Supplementary Report* agreed by a small majority. This recommended the 'termination' of the matter of the allegations against the Professor after "a long and intensive enquiry." How long and 'intensive' such an 'enquiry' could be within 21 days in these circumstances is a searching and significant point. It should be noted that no legal advice was sought regarding the three new complaints. A *Minority Report* was also presented desiring that the finding of the Training of the Ministry

---

[14] These are called *de recenti* statements in Scot's Law. See note 3 on page 28 below.

[15] Rev Alex MacDonald (Buccleuch and Greyfriars).

[16] Dr Murdoch Murchison (elder, Strathpeffer).

Committee with all relevant documents should go to the Edinburgh and Perth Presbytery for review and appropriate action (the rights of parties as to appeal, complaint or private actions to be preserved). In addition, a *Petition* was proposed by a minority asking the Assembly to instruct the Training of the Ministry Committee to make available all relevant documents and minutes necessary for the prosecution of a libel before the Presbytery of Edinburgh and Perth (always provided the complainants and witnesses were willing to cooperate). These Reports and the Petition duly went up to the 1995 General Assembly.[17]

The new complaints/allegations, then, were treated in the same way as the earlier ones. The claims of the women were thought in one way or another to be fanciful and merely of a 'one person's word against another' sort. The Professor himself was not questioned on these new allegations and notably chose not to request a libel on these matters in order to 'clear his name.'[18] Needless to say this made the matter hard to handle because of the polarisation of the Committee. At any rate two Reports and a Petition went up to the 1995 General Assembly, but still there was no *Case* in the Church Courts.

The General Assembly of 1995 (May 1995)

By this time there was a widespread *fama* on these matters both within the Church and in the public domain.[19] Third parties outside the Committee were aware of some of the issues involved, especially in England and Australia. There was therefore a strong feeling among some that a 'case' was required so that the matter might be dealt with decisively in the interests of all parties. It is true that the *Practice of the Free Church of Scotland* states that, "In all cases which may lead to a libel,

---

[17] It may be noted that the Committee never did seek legal advice on the additional allegations, nor did they initiate a citation to the Professor to ensure that he appeared before the Committee in relation to the additional allegations/complaints made.

[18] By contrast it is interesting that when a charge of inappropriate sexual conduct was raised by a woman against the revered John Macdonald in 1842 "he at once insisted on the matter being taken up by his presbytery" (John Kennedy, *The "Apostle of the North,"* London, 1866, 292). Macdonald was subsequently exonerated.

[19] A *fama* is a public report or rumour of a scandal.

a careful preliminary examination of proposed witnesses is requisite by the party prosecuting in order that a charge incapable of proof may not be proceeded with."[20] The question of capability of proof was real and had been a much disputed one within the Committee. However, as already indicated there were grounds for maintaining that all the requirements of the *Practice* had not been fulfilled.[21] It was not clear-cut, however, given the consistent position of three of the four special assessors, whose views should have carried some weight. Supposing there was no case ('libel') it was difficult to see how the *fama* could effectively be quietened, given a decision that the matter would not be pursued because it was thought to be incapable of proof. After all, such a decision would not itself establish *innocence*. Although the right of a person to be considered innocent until *proven* guilty was to be recognised, nonetheless there would remain the unchallenged *claims* of the women in question. They would simply suffer the uncontested counter-claims of their lack of credibility. By any measure the result could not but be unsatisfactory for the Church, not to speak of the parties involved in the matter. Furthermore, in the wider public perception, and even among many within the Church itself, there would very likely be a persisting suspicion of ranks being closed in the Church and there being something to hide. Furthermore, considering that both the police and the Crown Office subsequently thought the matter worthy of investigation under criminal law, concluding that there *was* a case to answer at law, makes it all the stranger that a Church with moral as well as spiritual issues to consider came to a different conclusion, albeit by a slender majority.

At any rate, a case was avoided, or evaded, at the 1995 Assembly by a motion approved by a majority, designed and intended to put an end to discussions on the matter. Because this was not a *judicial* decision – there being no Case – it was not realistic to expect

---

[20] *The Practice of the Free Church of Scotland in Her Several Courts*, Edinburgh, [8]1995, 107. This is the same as the wording in the previous edition of the *Practice* (1964), 90.
[21] See note 6 on page 15 above.

that it would have the effect of quietening the *fama* about the allegations, especially as by this time knowledge of the issue was known far and wide inside the Church, elsewhere among Christian Churches and even by the Press. Also, the Church was near evenly divided on the matter and a significant percentage of the membership of the Assembly dissented from the finding, possibly as many as 30%.[22] As far as the Church was concerned the motion – which may be considered objectionable in Church law – was framed as a quasi-judicial decision. However, there had been no case before it, and the women who had made allegations would not be heard by the Assembly, nor indeed, would the Professor's defence. The decision, however, subsequently came to be used as a 'stick' to beat down any unhappiness about the procedures adopted, as if it were judicial and inviolable, which actually it could not be (because there was no 'case' in the Church courts).

The finding of that 1995 Assembly in relation to the matter of allegations was as follows:

> On completion of a long and intensive enquiry into allegations made against Rev. Professor Donald Macleod, the Committee found no evidence capable of proving in the courts of the Church censurable conduct on the part of Rev. Professor Donald Macleod. Therefore the enquiry is completely terminated and no action is taken against Rev. Professor Donald Macleod.

In addition it was stated that: "the matter is now closed and...anyone seeking to pursue it further does so at the risk of themselves being censured as slanderers."[23] The General Assembly came to this finding, it has to be said, without most of the commissioners hearing or having sight of the necessary information regarding the allegations. It contained undefined allegations and investigations and was framed as if

---

[22] In a gathering of around 80 commissioners there were 27 dissents on the part of those who voted against the proposal put to the Assembly. In the event a 'swing' of only 5 or 6 votes would have seen a different result that day.

[23] This, it must be said, is consistent with the practice of the Church in connection with raising complaints and pursuing libels against others in the Church. See *Practice*, Edinburgh, [8]1995, 106-7.

it were a judicial decision, what with the statement about 'the matter' being closed, and threats against any who might conscientiously believe 'the matter' not to have been adequately handled. In any case it was unlikely to be implemented, given the fact that there could be a reasoned defence against slander, something the finding seemed to be designed to avoid! There was subsequent vocal disquiet over the 1995 decision. The 'closing' of a matter in such a manner, given the sharp division in the Church, and in view of so many 'loose ends', was by any measure distinctly 'unsafe.' The fact was that for the greater part those voting on this finding knew neither the specific allegations made, nor the charges, nor the nature of the investigations. Dissent[24] from the finding was recorded by 27 Commissioners, a significant percentage of those present, perhaps as much as a third of those voting.

Flaws in the Finding of the 1995 Assembly

This finding of the 1995 Assembly in relation to the allegations against the Professor contained what may be considered as serious flaws, especially in that the General Assembly was not informed that all the requirements regarding a careful preliminary examination of witnesses had not been fulfilled. In addition to this there are the following considerations:

(1)   On the one hand, it stated that in the matter of the allegations there was "no evidence capable of proof." Was it a charge incapable of proof? One problem in these instances is that such alleged incidents are not witnessed by third parties. But are there other witnesses who provide some corroboration? Are the complainants themselves and those to whom they told their stories credible? Are there no criteria by which such complaints can ever be addressed judicially, for the sake of both defendants and complainants? At any rate, it was the responsibility of the Committee to make the preliminary examination, to raise questions of the capability of proof, and

---

[24] See note 10 above.

to dismiss what might be trivial or even mischievous by way of allegation.[25] The Supplementary Report to the 1995 General Assembly denied that the principle of cumulative evidence from multiple individual witnesses to separate but related allegations was accepted in Free Church disciplinary procedures. However, the case of *Alexander Cant Kay* Free Church minister in Loanhead, Midlothian, in 1880, for example, showed that this was not the case. In that case individual witnesses of that minister's alleged intoxication through drugs or drink were considered to amount to cumulative evidence or corroboration of the alleged offence justifying judicial action.[26] Kay was suspended from the functions of the ministry and loosed from his pastoral charge on the basis of such evidence. Whatever sympathy one might have for this poor man, given that he seemed to have become addicted to a substance he believed (it was said) helped a medical condition, the proceedings in the case serve as a precedent for the allowance of cumulative evidence as sufficient to sustain a discipline case. In the matter of the allegations against the Professor, none of the complainants or those in whom they confided changed their stories or complaints, under close examination or enquiry, either in the Church or subsequently. In the instances before the Committee the capability of proof was clearly a contentious issue. The Committee had to take account of the cumulative evidence of a plurality of complainants, as well as the opinions of the special assessors appointed by the General Assembly. The five complainants involved were prepared, notwithstanding awkwardness to themselves, to present what they considered to be the truth of their allegations. In addition,

[25] *Practice*, Edinburgh, [8]1995, 107.
[26] *Proceedings and Debates of the General Assembly of the Free Church of Scotland*, Edinburgh, 1880, 26-37. Mr Kay, who had been ordained at Loanhead in 1863, subsequently immigrated to Canada.

some of their allegations were supported by statements from close friends who were prepared to confirm that the complainants had told them what had happened in the incidents in question. They might have raised a private libel individually, though they must at least have thought initially that it was sufficient to present their complaints to the Committee. After the 1995 decision private libels were going to be difficult to pursue through the Church, given the force of the 1995 finding. In any case the fact is that the finding of the General Assembly in 1995 could not strictly speaking be a *declaration of innocence*, and therefore could not *itself* quieten any *fama*, though some seemed to believe that that should have been its effect.

(2) On the other hand, the finding maintained that 'the matter' (never a 'case' in the Free Church courts) was "completely terminated." Later, in June 1999, this was strengthened when it was stated that the 'matter' concerning the allegations against the Professor was not to be pursued *"in any form whatsoever."* To this was added an accompanying caveat that if the matter was raised formally those who raised such action would open themselves up to censure for slander if their case was not proven. This became a serious issue in relation to the matter of the allegations against the Professor. Such a finding (of 1995) was used as a disciplinary tool, *as if it were part of the constitution to which the Church adhered.* It was just authoritarianism - arbitrary Church 'law' – and an unwarranted 'gagging order' on its office bearers. This is not to say that office bearers may be *dis*respectful of the proper authority or decisions of the highest court of the Church. However, the highest court of the Church ought to operate within the constitutional and disciplinary framework of the Church and not in a merely authoritarian way. In this case a very high percentage of the membership of the General Assembly in 1995 dissented from the finding. The

fact was that the finding was distinctly 'unsafe.' In the end this was a significant element in the unhappy subsequent polarisation and then division in the Church.

Among reasons for dissent recorded in relation to the decision of the Assembly were the following from those who had presented a Petition on the matter:

> (1) The minority were given no means by which the substance of the matter they dissented from could be reviewed by Church Courts,
>
> (2) The matter had been closed without the basic evidence being examined by the Courts of the Church,
>
> (3) The basic Presbyterial procedures whereby a *fama clamosa*[27] can be quietened and the innocence of the innocent established had not been allowed to be fulfilled.
>
> (4) Committee decisions which established precedents, now stood without a review of their substance by a Court of the Church.[28]

Inevitably, given the almost evenly divided state of the Church on the issue – and although at that time there was little evidence of a merely partisan spirit – there was a continuing underlying feeling among many that the 'matter' had not been satisfactorily handled in strict fairness to all parties involved.

---

[27] A *Fama clamosa* is 'an aggravated report of a scandal.'

[28] This dissent was adhered to by Ronald C Christie, Gordon Mair, Hugh M Cartwright, John W Keddie and Wilfred Weale. The purpose of the petition had been to obtain papers of the Committee in relation to the allegations with a view to pursuing a separate libel, if thought appropriate. In the event the Petition failed consequent upon the final decision of the Assembly.

COURT CASE AND ITS AFTERMATH
1996-1999

It is understandable and perhaps even obvious that the women in this country who had made allegations of improper conduct towards them on the Professor's part should be extremely unhappy at the outcome of things within the Church. Where did that leave them and their allegations? They had approached the Church because they felt that the behaviour of which they complained was unbecoming a minister of religion and should be made known to the appropriate church authorities to the end that others might be protected from what they had experienced. This point was not really appreciated by the majority in the Committee and the women found their credibility rather easily dismissed. Several of the five women were professing Christians and members in the Church. They understandably felt let down by the Church. Some of the women in question independently decided to go to the police with their complaints. Some of the complainants were contacted directly by the police, and also other women who did not appear in Court. Some felt that serious criminal actions were involved which they felt it to be their duty to report to the authorities. Others had information which they felt might be relevant as evidence of criminality.

The Case at Law
The police enquiry subsequently submitted to the Procurator Fiscal clearly maintained that there *was* a case to answer.[1] The Procurator Fiscal was responsible for laying the charges. The *Procurator Fiscal* decided that the matter was serious enough and the evidence strong enough to move to a Court case. This, then, was a criminal case raised

---

[1] It should be noted that the allegations investigated by the police did *not* include the allegation from Australia, which did not involve a criminal matter.

by the Crown and heard in a criminal court. It was not an action raised by the women themselves, but raised on the basis of information supplied by them. A case was therefore subsequently raised in the Sheriff Court in Edinburgh alleging sexual assault on the part of the Free Church College Professor. The case involved the application of the 'Moorov' principle whereby actions of a repetitive kind of the same nature involving different people amounted to cumulative evidence against the accused.[2] In such cases it is expected that the complainant at some point shortly after the event spoke about the experience to a friend or confidant. This is usually termed a *de recenti* statement. It is not taken as *corroboration* of the event but usually is taken as a strong support of the credibility of the complainant. It appears that in this case the *de recenti* support for the complaints was not presented in the court. It clearly should have been. The failure to do that weakened the strength of the case.[3] It is of significance that the alleged 'conspirators' were not

---

[2] 'Moorov doctrine' is taken from *Moorov v HM Advocate* 1930 JC 68. Cf.: "One of the distinctive features of Scots criminal law is the requirement of corroboration: with a very few statutory exceptions, no criminal charge may be proved unless each crucial fact is established by evidence from more than one source. The *Moorov* doctrine represents what might at first sight appear to be an exception to this requirement by permitting the credible but uncorroborated evidence of a single witness to an offence to corroborate, and to be corroborated by, the credible but uncorroborated evidence of a single witness to another offence. Such mutual corroboration is only permitted where the crimes are sufficiently connected in time, character and circumstance. What constitutes a sufficient connection has been the matter of extensive discussion in the courts. Logically, the *Moorov* doctrine is an example of the admissibility of similar fact evidence." (From *Scots Law Commission Report*, Report on Similar Fact Evidence and the Moorov Doctrine, May 2012, 1.7, pages 2-3).
(See http://www.scotlawcom.gov.uk/files/5813/3767/3532/rep229.pdf. Accessed 27 September 2016).
[3] "At common law evidence may be led of a statement made by a witness shortly after the occurrence. Such evidence is not corroboration of the fact of the occurrence. Its only effect, if the statement tallies with the witness's evidence, is to enhance the witness's credibility, by showing that his story has been the same from the beginning. Although such evidence may theoretically be admissible in any case, it is tendered mainly in cases of physical injury…Evidence of a *de recenti* statement by an accused person has been admitted for the purpose of showing that the person's story has been consistent" (Walker and Walker: *The Law of Evidence in Scotland*, 3rd Edition, Bloomsbury Professional, 2009, 8.3.1-8.3.2).

called as witnesses and the prosecution was not in possession of Church documents which were used selectively in the trial by the Defence.

Naturally a case like this created considerable interest in a press all too keen to expose scandal in a Church, especially of a prurient nature. It is even mentioned in a major contemporary history of 'Scotland's Twentieth Century'![4] The details of this case, as well as the intriguing and ultimately successful defence of 'Conspiracy' against the said Professor, involving personnel within the Free Church and beyond, has been well documented in the book of Murdoch Murchison and Iain Murray, *When Justice Failed in Church and State*.[5] This book is critical of the procedures in the Church and Criminal courts and a substantially accurate account of the whole issue. That it not to say it is beyond criticism in some particulars. The official Free Church web-site posted a review by one of its ministers who raised issues of fact and interpretation in the book. These, however, as much as anything tended simply to underline the inadequacies of the *presentation* rather than the substance of the prosecution's case.[6]

Suffice to say that the Professor was acquitted in that Court. However, not everyone by any means concurred with the judgement. The Sheriff did not accept the credibility of the women whose allegations were at the heart of the prosecution case. For him, it appears, the explanation for their willingness to raise such allegations lay in his supposition, which he stated as such, that this was a result of a *campaign*. It was reported in the press that, "in his review of the

---

[4] See Catriona M M Macdonald, *Whaur Extremes Meet*, Edinburgh, 2009, 286-7.

[5] Murdoch Murchison and Iain H Murray, *When Justice Failed in Church and State*, privately published, 2001. The sub-title of this 88-page paperback is 'An Explanation of the Division in the Free Church of Scotland.' It is by and large a fair and accurate account of the whole matter, though an unofficial statement of what were perceived to be inadequacies in the procedures both in the Church and in the Sheriff Court actions.

[6] See the review by David Robertson dated 25 May 2001 and posted on the official Free Church web-site: http://www.freechurch.org/issues/2001/may01b.htm (since removed). There has, however, to date been no official response to *When Justice Failed in Church and State*.

evidence, Sheriff Horsburgh said: 'I have come to the conclusion that there was a campaign against him.'" He accepted an accusation that some members of the Training of the Ministry Committee had been "conducting a vendetta."[7] The result and the statements made publicly by the Sheriff in support of his verdict not only impugned the character of the women in whose names the case had been raised, but also impugned the reputation of many men assumed to be conspirators though they had been given no opportunity to speak for themselves.

In essence, the prosecution in the 1996 court case was unable to counter most of the points raised for the defence on account of the following factors:

(1.) It was handicapped in that it had not obtained the Training of the Ministry Committee documents relating to the investigations into the allegations against Professor Macleod, whereas the defence team had obtained the documents by court order in January 1996. Only a few of the Training of the Ministry documents obtained by the defence were produced in court. This meant, for example, that the Prosecution was not in possession of the following:

(a.) the interviews of the complainants by the Church;

(b.) the interviews of Professor Macleod by the Church;

(c.) the statements of the *de recenti* witnesses.

(2.) It failed to bring before the court any *de recenti* witnesses themselves to support the testimony of the complainants.

(3.) It failed to call any of the alleged conspirators.

It appears that the prosecution underestimated the complexity of the case which may have appeared clear-cut. However, it is only fair to say that the Procurator Fiscal involved in the case took it up at very short notice due to resources which had to be put in to the Dunblane enquiry that summer.

---

[7] *The Daily Telegraph*, Wednesday, June 26 1996.

A conspiracy?

For the Church this claim of a 'campaign' or 'conspiracy' was a bit of a disaster, to put it mildly. Many in the Church were of course pleased with an acquittal for the Professor. However, it was at a serious cost. After all, it left the question: what about the supposed perverse 'campaign' or 'vendetta' that was so persuasive to the Sheriff? Who was involved in it? Furthermore, given the assumption of a conspiracy by many within the Church (and beyond), was it not the duty of the Church to root them out and censure them?[8]

An implication of the verdict was that the women in question had perjured themselves, a criminal offence which might conceivably have landed them in serious trouble. Normally the Crown Office deals harshly with lying in Court. However, after a six-week period in which that question was investigated the Crown Office stated:

> After considering a Report by the Procurator Fiscal at Edinburgh into the trial of Professor Donald MacLeod, Crown Counsel have concluded that no further investigations are warranted and that criminal proceedings against the witnesses would not be justified.
> The Report was requested by the Lord Advocate to establish whether there were grounds for instituting proceedings for perjury against any of the witnesses who gave evidence at the trial or for conspiracy to pervert the course of justice.[9]

This statement covers two aspects of the case. It is clear that the Crown Office was persuaded on the one hand that there were *no grounds for instituting proceedings for perjury* against witnesses who gave evidence in the trial. It is also clear that it saw *no grounds for pursuing the suggestion that there*

---

[8] The *Form of Process* states regarding a *fama clamosa*: "That the *fama clamosa* of the scandal be so great, as that the presbytery, for their own vindication, see themselves necessitate to begin the process, without any particular accuser; but the presbytery in this case should be careful, first to inquire into the rise, occasion, broachers, and grounds of this *fama clamosa.*" See *Practice*, Edinburgh, [8]1995, 191. This, however, the Church signally failed to do.

[9] Statement issued by the Crown Office, dated August 7, 1996. This followed remarks made by Sheriff John Horsburgh Q.C. in Edinburgh Sheriff Court on June 25, 1996 at the conclusion of Professor Macleod's trial.

may have been a conspiracy to pervert the course of justice.[10] On this matter, however, the Church was silent. No doubt it would have been awkward, even anomalous, for the Church to express any thanksgiving that the witnesses in question, some of whom were members or adherents in the Church, or supposed conspirators, would not be charged with perjury or any conspiracy to pervert the course of justice because no grounds were found for doing so! Another irony in the issue was that, should there have been a trial for perjury a different story might have emerged, in which case perjury might have been demonstrated on the other side. How conscious the Free Church was of such a scenario is unclear.

A striking feature in this whole matter was the refusal of the Free Church to provide relevant papers to the police when requested for them. This showed a lack of willingness to co-operate with the civil authorities in matters which, if true, involved criminal offences. If such information had been supplied it would, in effect, have made the defence of 'campaign' or 'conspiracy' all the more difficult to sustain![11] Furthermore, if such information had been released *after* the Court case it might well have emerged that there were contradictions between the defendant's evidence in Court and information provided to the Training of the Ministry Committee. This was all part of what were considered by some to be unsatisfactory processes on this matter within the Free Church itself.

The Fallout in the Church – 1996

The implications for the Church of this decision were far-reaching. The problem arose from the Sheriff's stated acceptance of the idea of a 'campaign' within the Church to bring down the Professor. This actually had several implications:

---

[10] This was confirmed by the Law Officers' Secretariat in a letter to the Rev John MacLeod (Tarbat) dated 9th August 1996.
[11] It may be noted that the Procurator Fiscal could of course have obtained the relevant documents by court order had she wished to do so. The fact that she did not do so clearly weakened the case.

- If the Professor allowed a 'defence' of such a campaign, did he not have the responsibility to raise that in the Church courts against those whom he considered had conspired with the complainants against him?

- The Church was faced with the dilemma that it could not have things both ways: it could not, on the one hand, have delight at an acquittal, and on the other hand have accusations of conspiracy against ministers and elders of the Church left unaddressed. After all, that was arguably as serious an offence, if established, as what had been originally alleged against the Professor.

- Furthermore, the Church was faced with the serious hiatus that there could hardly be 'acquittal' and 'no conspiracy' at the same time, given that 'conspiracy,' essentially, was the accepted basis of the acquittal. Having said this it is only fair to say that the Sheriff made it clear that his decision was based on the credibility of the witnesses. However, he did accept that the reason he believed that the women were not credible was that they had been persuaded to make the allegations against the Professor by others who had a vested interest in, presumably, 'bringing him down.'

This matter came up in the regular Commission of Assembly on 2nd October 1996. Some members of the Commission recognised the dilemma in which the church was placed. Whilst delight was felt that there had been an acquittal in the Sheriff Court, there were some who were not so delighted, because of what were seen to be serious flaws in the conduct of the Court action. Some felt that the women had been badly treated, and that the Church was under the spotlight on account of the 'conspiracy' defence. In the interests of righteousness, and the public perception of conspiratorial actions of some (or many) within the Church, the matter of 'conspiracy' required to be investigated and addressed. However, within the Church it was widely believed that the conspiracy notion was fatuous and unsupportable. Obviously, an examination finding such a thing would throw serious doubt on the soundness of the defence in the Sheriff Court case and therefore on its decision. And so the Commission of October 1996 was a crux for the Church. In point of fact the Commissions of 1996 were a turning point for the Church in that they perpetuated a distinct polarisation within the denomination which led to the division of 2000.

Polarisation in the Church – The First October Commission, 1996

The first Commission of October 1996 was a 'hotchpotch' of conflicting concerns. It expressed thanks for the acquittal of the Professor in the Sheriff Court. It also set up an investigative Committee to enquire about certain ministers in Committees who had allegedly 'lost the confidence of many in the Church.' In addition, the Training of the Ministry Committee was directed to investigate various reported statements and comments from Professor Donald Macleod considered to be at variance with the Church's confessional position.

Also, controversially and at odds with the thanks for the acquittal of the Professor, there was a statement that the Commission repudiated 'the idea that there had been such a conspiracy', i.e. to pervert the course of justice in the case of the Professor in the Sheriff Court.[12] It is fair to say that this acted like an incendiary bomb in the Church.

Five days after the Commission a meeting objecting to the decisions of the Commission was held at Perth apparently attended by 46 ministers and 42 elders, with apologies from a further 15 ministers. This was reported as a 'private' meeting, though it made a very public statement endorsing a 'memorial' to be signed by willing parties throughout the Church and calling for another Commission to rescind the decisions of the previous one. This 'memorial' manifested an unwillingness or unpreparedness to accept any unhappiness in the Church at the outcome of the Sheriff Court on account of the implicit

---

[12] There were 17 dissents from the final decision of the 1st Commission in October 1996, none with reasons.

accusation of conspiracy within the Church. The 'memorial' further expressed an unwillingness or unpreparedness to recognise the unsettling nature of statements and comments made by the Professor which were considered by some to be at odds with ordination vows. Such a petition inevitably was a divisive instrument. It effectively promoted a Macleod defence movement. Its immediate effect was the successful engineering of a call for another Commission to be held.

Meantime in a 'Front Page Footnotes' in the *West Highland Free Press* issue of Friday, 11 October 1996, Donald Macleod wrote at length on the First October Commission. The acerbic tone of the article is indicated sufficiently by the somewhat sensational title: 'The lunatics have taken over the Free Church asylum.' Pretty well every aspect of the Commission's decisions is criticised by the Professor. He also maintained that there *was* a conspiracy – against himself – in the Church: "I categorically reject the idea there was no conspiracy..." In criticising those involved, some of whom he named, he concluded the article with a hyperbole: "Their actions will resonate to dishonour of Christianity for centuries"! One suspects that succeeding centuries would, if anything, be more likely to remember the headline of this front-page article than any decisions of the October 1996 Commission of an insignificant little Church in Scotland!

In an interesting irony, the title of the article alone made the later remarks of Maurice Roberts in the 1999 Assembly, *for which he was disciplined*, somewhat tame by comparison. The Professor certainly had a right to defend himself. He would have had opportunity for that through the Church courts. But it was, to say the least, questionable to resort to the use of the privilege of a regular newspaper column within the public domain in doing so. Among other things it is unfortunate that in the article he repeated the inaccurate statement that the Convener of the Committee "rubbed his hands in glee and said, 'We've got him now!'"[13]

---

[13] The author was present when the alleged event – "according to one witness" – took place and can confirm that the remarks had to do with the form of words for a finding

The Second October Commission, 1996

As a consequence of the agitation the Moderator was prevailed upon to call another Commission. As a result, on 31st October a Commission duly met and by a slender majority rescinded the findings of the earlier Commission. In the end, however, it made no decisive statements at all, contenting itself with two grand sounding but rather innocuous statements, one about the promotion of reconciliation (without specifying just exactly what 'reconciliation' was required and how it should be practically achieved) and the other stating recognition "that as a Church we have failed in our attempts to deal in a God-glorifying way with the problems facing the Church" (without specifying exactly what the 'problems' were). This was sufficiently vague to satisfy most commissioners, but it made no contribution to the resolution of the clear polarisation that was now evident in the Church.[14] It was also a remarkable statement given the weight that was subsequently put on the 1995 'Finding' in the matter, the purported decisiveness of which seemed to be seriously compromised by this finding of the Commission of 31st October 1996, given the concession that the matter had not been dealt with in a God-glorifying manner.

'Professor Donald Macleod and His "Opponents"' (1996)

In October 1996, the Rev. Iain H. Murray, who had been assumed to be a 'chief conspirator' in the actions involving the Professor, published a booklet with the above title. Iain Murray was a much-respected figure in the Reformed constituency. Whilst he had been a minister without charge in the Free Church for a few years in the 1970s his main influence among the churches was through his editorial work and publications with the Banner of Truth Trust. He was aware of issues that had arisen both in Australia and in the United Kingdom in the

---

of the Committee – an 'it' – and not the Professor himself.

[14] Though no dissents were recorded in relation to the final decision of the Commission of 31st October 1996, there were 19 dissents from a finding that this was a validly called meeting of the Commission and at a later stage there were seven dissents from a finding that it was competent to rescind the finding of the meeting of 2nd October.

matter of allegations against the Professor. His publication was a riposte to the innuendo involving his character which had been highlighted in the Sheriff Court action. The publication also effectively questioned the adequacy of the evidence produced in the Court action and provided evidence which undermined the counter-allegations of conspiracy, with which he was believed to be involved. It disclosed the facts that (1) key witnesses had not been questioned by the Church; and (2) at least most of the complainants in the court had *de recenti* witnesses who were never heard in the Sheriff Court.

This publication received a wide circulation. Based on its contents representations were made to the Training of the Ministry Committee. Some members of the Committee brought the matter to the 1997 General Assembly but were duly 'censured' and summarily removed from the Committee for raising matters considered to have been decisively closed by the 1995 Assembly finding. However, the work was instrumental in bringing a critique of the Church procedures and the Sheriff Court decision into the public domain, to the discomfort of the Church it must be said.[15]

The escalation of conflict – 1997-1998

There is no doubt that the 'private' Perth meeting after the first October Commission exacerbated the polarisation within the Church. It was not just that there was continuing dissatisfaction felt by many about the outcome or aftermath of the Sheriff Court action of the summer of 1996. There were also deep concerns about statements made by Professor Macleod in the pages of the *West Highland Free Press* and other journals or broadcasts. The trouble was that such was the support for the Professor that it seemed that he was beyond censure. As a result of the Perth meeting of 7th October 1996 a pressure group known as *Free Concern* was organised. This organisation produced a Newsletter before the 1997 General Assembly. Though it stated its aim

---

[15] Iain Murray's booklet subsequently appeared as the second chapter in *When Justice Failed in Church and State* which was published in April 2001.

as a uniting one, they must have realised that it would have the effect of producing a reaction among those not persuaded by the soundness of the decision of the Church or in the law court in the matter. It was widely recognised in the Church that there were underlying tensions on constitutional, traditional and worship matters. *Free Concern* was without doubt the catalyst in the escalation of polarisation and division in the Church. In 1997 a group of counter-concerned Free Church ministers, elders and people re-organised a *Free Church Defence Association*. The irony is that it is possible that had 'Free Concern' not been organised the FCDA might not have been re-organised.

An FCDA had been organised in the Free Church by James Begg among others in 1870 during the first union controversy involving the Free and United Presbyterian Churches. This had become effectively defunct when that controversy ended in 1873. However, an FCDA was re-activated in 1898 at the height of the second union controversy which resulted in the United Free Church in 1900 and a minority Free Church continuing thereafter. One of the ironies in the controversy in the Free Church a century later was the fact that *Free Concern* also considered itself an FCDA. In its newsletter of May 1997, it was claimed that "in effect *Free Concern* is a Free Church Defence Association." Given what happened two years later in the decisions of the majority in the church courts in relation to the FCDA, this claim and the impact of the *Free Concern* movement were conveniently overlooked. The constitution of the reorganised FCDA was identical with the original organisation and was set for the defence of the constitutional and doctrinal principles of the Disruption Church. No formal disciplinary action was ever contemplated in the old Free Church against this 'free association' of like-minded devoted Free Churchmen and it was not anticipated that any such action would be contemplated against the new manifestation either. In the event, this was to prove seriously mistaken.

The newly organised FCDA had a fair amount of support and embarked upon a periodical magazine – quarterly – entitled the *Free*

Church Foundations, under the editorship of William Macleod, the Portree minister at the time. This magazine presented critical and penetrating reviews of the sorts of trends which were considered to have become evident within the Free Church. It was felt that the Free Church was drifting from the constitutional moorings of the old Church. The articles in the magazine were unattributed but many of them stirred up a strong reaction amongst those committed to change in the Church – what might be described as the modernising elements. However, it was perhaps no surprise that when in 1999 the balance of votes in the highest court of the Church – the General Assembly (and its Commission(s)) – fell in favour of what may be called the *Free Concern* faction,[16] action was contemplated against the FCDA *qua* FCDA as an organisation allegedly subversive of the harmony of the Church and encouraging a divisive course, though in fact it simply reflected an already existing disharmony.[17]

'Special Commission to seek Reconciliation' (1998)

At the 1998 Assembly Overtures came up to the Assembly from the Presbytery of Caithness and Sutherland and from the floor of the Assembly, the laudable intent of which was to seek Reconciliation between estranged parties within the Church. The Special Commission comprised the Assembly Clerks together with Presbytery Clerks and the Moderator of the 1998 General Assembly (Rev. D. K. Macleod). Church Courts and Committees were instructed to cooperate with the Commission to promote reconciliation. In addition, individuals were invited to make representations in writing. In terms of time-scale, Presbytery returns were to be submitted to the Commission of

---

[16] *Free Concern* had disbanded by 1999.

[17] In its pleadings in the Court of Session action of 2004 the Free Church argued that the FCDA before 1900 had not adopted an agenda against an individual, as distinct from the post-1997 FCDA. However, the issues taken up involved principles and the basis of righteous action within the Church. No doubt in its pre-1900 manifestation the FCDA would have been accused of focussing critically on the character and actions of individuals, such as, for example, Principal Robert Rainy.

Assembly of October 1998, with a view to calling for a Plenary
Assembly not later than December 1998.[18] "The aim of the Plenary
Assembly," stated the Act of May 1998, "shall be to effect an
honourable reconciliation between estranged sections of our Church
and thus enable us unitedly to prosecute the Great Commission."[19]

The Special Commission faced real difficulties in carrying out
its remit in three main considerations: (1) the time scale was much too
short; (2) the remit in the Act required the Commission to remind
correspondents to the Commission of "the embargo imposed by the
Deliverance of the 1995 Assembly" (that is to say in the matter of
allegations against the Professor); and (3) the way and manner in which
real concerns might be addressed and not evaded, thus encouraging all
too superficial attempts at 'reconciliation.'

It was well known that the '1995 Act' was an issue for many.
But so were well reported reasonable concerns on Church doctrine and
practice, as it was thought, in statements made by Professor Donald
Macleod in the public domain in recent times and which some wished
to see examined. It would therefore appear to those for whom it was a
concern that this non-negotiable aspect of the remit would likely
scupper the aim of the Special Commission. It was clearly challenging
to frame any proposals which would be decisive. It would also be
difficult to prevent the party which had a majority of the votes (as in
1995) from being suppressive or even oppressive of the minority
section in this whole matter. This proved to be the case in this instance.

'Reconciliation' was a grand aim. It proved elusive. In this case
it would require the minority to act against convictions about

---

[18] A *Plenary Assembly* is one in which all members of all Presbyteries are entitled to be
representatives at a General Assembly, or such elders from amongst their congregations
who are able to attend if Presbytery elders are unable to do so. This will normally be
arranged by agreement of all Presbyteries under the Barrier Act, an Act of 1697, a
provision which prevents the General Assembly from taking decisions which might
profoundly affect the polity of the Church without first referring these to the
Presbyteries.

[19] *Principal Acts of the General Assembly of the Free Church of Scotland*, Act appointing Special
Commission to seek Reconciliation, (No. 16 of Class 2, May, 1998).

righteousness. It was all very well to speak of a desire for reconciliation. Reconciliation itself, however, cannot in the nature of the case be achieved irrespective of righteous concerns. But this all emerged in the discussions and in the motions on the matter when discussion of the Report of the Special Commission finally came before the Commission of Assembly in June, 1999. Lack of time had meant that the Report was not taken up at the General Assembly that May.

Private Libels raised

It is clear from the *Practice* of the Free Church that parties other than a Presbytery can raise a libel against a minister for what are considered to be breaches of the ordination vows of such a minister.[20] The Libel will state (1) the nature of the alleged offence; (2) the assertion of the guilt of the accused minister with relevant facts and documentation in support of the allegations; and (3) a conclusion stating the guilt of the offence mentioned and therefore a requirement for the application of proper disciplinary action. Although the Training of the Ministry Committee is charged with originating and prosecuting processes against a Professor, the *Practice* states that "The rights competent to all parties according to the laws of the Church are at the same time reserved."[21] This preserves the right of a private individual to bring a libel before the Presbytery irrespective of the functions conferred on the Training of the Ministry Committee.[22]

In relation to the 1998 General Assembly one onlooker recalled that "In the 1998 Assembly, at which I was a visitor, I heard with my own ears the leaders of the Assembly say that if anyone felt they had evidence against Professor (now Principal) Macleod the way to go ahead was to take a Private Libel against him. It was made clear that no one is above the law of the Church."[23] In the ensuing months

---

[20] *Practice of the Free Church of Scotland*, Edinburgh, [8]1995, 106-111. See especially sections 2.20 and 2.26.

[21] ibid., 2.11, 107.

[22] ibid., 2.9 and 2.10, 106-107.

[23] Rev. Maurice Roberts, 'Hypocrisy and Wickedness in the 1999 Assembly,' in, *Free*

several ministers drew up Libels to present to the Edinburgh Presbytery: Rev. Maurice Roberts (Inverness)(on breach of ordination vows regarding purity of worship); Rev. John Harding (Shettleston)(on dishonesty in the civil court); Rev. David Murray (Lochcarron)(on slander against named ministers and an elder at the Sheriff Court trial of 1996); and Rev. William Macleod (Portree)(on breaches of the 9th Commandment). These were lodged with the Edinburgh Presbytery on 16th March 1999, and the Presbytery's Committee on Bills and Overtures reported to a full meeting of Presbytery on 30th March. The Committee recommended that the Libels be not passed in to the Presbytery, essentially on technicalities. In particular, they could see no evidence that the accused minister had been informed beforehand of the intended Libels nor that the libellers had taken *complaints* to the Presbytery or Training of the Ministry Committee. They were therefore not received into the Presbytery.

Though the libellers appealed to Synod, the Synod dismissed the appeals, as did the General Assembly on 12th May 1999. The Assembly went as far as to "ordain that this matter be now terminated."[24] Whilst 'technicalities' are by no means unimportant in disciplinary matters, it is a shame that the matters of *substance* in the Libels were not so much as discussed, especially given that so much of the detail was already in the public domain by then and numerous complaints had been submitted to Church committees and courts, not least letters of concern in connection with Iain H. Murray's post-1995 *Professor Donald Macleod and His 'Opponents.'* It is true to say that the libellers themselves recognised that the voting pattern in the Presbytery (and the other Church Courts that year) pretty well ensured that such matters of substance would not come before Church judicatories.[25] That also seemed to be sealed by the authoritarian rider in the decision of May

---

Church Foundations, Special June Commission of Assembly Issue, August, 1999, 8.
[24] *Acts and Proceedings of the General Assembly of the Free Church of Scotland*, May 1999, 54-57.
[25] See the article 'Libels Rejected' in the magazine of the FCDA, *Free Church Foundations*, July 1999, 3-5.

1999 that "this matter be now terminated," without defining "this matter" nor hearing any Libels!

Hence, on 12th May 1999, the General Assembly seemingly closed the door on any attempts at Private Libels.[26] It was that decision which was the context for the statement of Maurice Roberts to which such exception was taken later in that same Assembly, as we shall see.

Western Synod – April 1999

A distinct catalyst in the escalation of division within the Church was the decision of the minister of the Stornoway congregation (Rev. Kenneth Stewart) initially to invite Professor Donald Macleod, Rev. Angus Smith (Ness, Lewis) and Rev. Wilfred Weale (Ullapool) to the February 1999 Communion. The idea, it seems, was to try to encourage some rapprochement among the perceived diverse factions in the Church. On the face of it, though plausible, this was not a very wise decision. At any rate, it misfired as Smith and Weale both withdrew from the Communion. What exacerbated the situation was the withdrawal initially of a number of members and adherents from the Free Church congregation to worship separately as a group which became known as 'Stornoway Reformed Fellowship.' Those attached to the Fellowship absented themselves from the Communion services of the congregation. This 'reaction' was not beyond criticism, though the situation was one of unusually heightened feelings. At any rate, the men were acted against promptly by the Stornoway Kirk Session, as a result of which they were threatened with excommunication as 'schismatics.'

As required by the *Practice* the Kirk Session referred the matter to the Presbytery which advised discipline if, after a further meeting, the

---

[26] This decision was consolidated later by the Commission of Assembly in June 1999, in which the following was passed: "Therefore, the Commission of Assembly *declare* that any opportunity for private action in regard to this matter in the courts of the Church now ceases." Among reasons for dissent lodged against this finding was the following: "It is incompetent in that it is improper and unconstitutional for the Commission to impose a prohibition or interdict on any action to which the *Form of Process* gives a right." Quite so. It was simply crass authoritarianism.

accused men did not return to the Stornoway congregation.[27] The
accused men then appealed to the Western Synod held in Stornoway on
13th April 1999. With the Free Presbytery of Lewis at the bar[28], the
other two Presbyteries within the Synod [Skye and Uist, and
Lochcarron] on the face of it unanimously (in that there was no counter
motion) made a reasonable decision to put the matter back to the Free
Presbytery of Lewis to instruct the congregation and minister of
Stornoway to deal with the issue more pastorally. The finding was quite
comprehensive and was in truth sensitive to all parties in the
circumstances:

> The Synod sustain the Appeal by Messrs [names of the
> appellants omitted here] against the finding of the Free
> Presbytery of Lewis reached on 30th March 1999 and
> rescind the judgment of the Free Presbytery of Lewis. The
> Synod note:
> 1. The difficulties on the part of Rev. Kenneth Stewart to
> discuss in a pastoral context the substance of the concern
> over the invitation to Prof. D. Macleod.
> 2. The absence of extract minutes from the Kirk Session
> records in the hands of the appellants prior to Kirk Session
> meetings and Presbytery meeting, despite requests for them.
> 3. The introduction of the sanction to remove the names of
> the appellants from the Communion Roll at an early stage in
> the discussions when other avenues involving a lesser
> sanction had not been fully exhausted.

---

[27] The Stornoway Kirk Session readily invoked the *Form of Process* in pursuing
disciplinary action against these men for schism. (*Practice*, Edinburgh, [8]1995, 190
(Chapter VI, Section 1 of the *Form*)). Neither the Kirk Session nor the Presbytery,
however, seemed to recognise that Section 2 of the same Chapter in the *Form* required
that: "When there is no confession of the scandals..., the session are not to proceed to
lead probation by witnesses or presumptions, till an account of the matter be brought
by reference to the presbytery..., and the presbytery do thereupon appoint the session to
proceed and lead probation; and after probation is led, the same is to be brought to the
presbytery, who may inflict what censure they see cause." 'Probation' simply means,
generally, 'trial.' The fact that probation was never 'led' in the manner laid down in the
Form meant that the men in question were never really afforded an adequate
opportunity to defend themselves.
[28] This is a legal term which refers to parties in a case before Church Courts – accused
or accusers – being required to sit separately from those judging a case or a dispute.

4. The apparent lack of time to adequately prepare between the citing of the appellants and the meeting of the Kirk Session a few days later, before which they were to appear. Wherefore the Synod instruct the Free Presbytery of Lewis to instruct the Minister and Session of Stornoway Free Church to commence a pastoral dialogue with the appellants to give an opportunity for the appellants to present their concerns over the invitation to Prof. D. Macleod and to seek a resolution of this matter which will retain the unity of the congregation and the valued membership of the appellants within it.

This was an invitation to give some 'breathing space' in the tense situation in which, it seemed to the representatives of the Skye and Uist and Lochcarron Presbyteries, the situation needed to be de-fused, given the unusual circumstances of the day.[29] However, in the event the Free Presbytery of Lewis was not of a mind for any 'breathing space.' It did not acquiesce in the decision and appealed to the May Assembly so that the original discipline administered in the Stornoway congregation might be endorsed. That was precisely what happened at the General Assembly in May.

The decision of the Assembly on 14th May, 1999, was as follows: "It was moved, seconded and agreed that: The General Assembly sustain the Appeal of the Presbytery of Lewis and reverse the judgment of the Western Synod. The General Assembly endorse the legality of the action of the Stornoway Kirk Session and extend encouragement to the Minister and Kirk Session of the Stornoway Congregation in the difficulties in which they have been engulfed. The General Assembly further commend the Presbytery of Lewis for their support in maintaining discipline within the congregation. The General Assembly direct the Kirk Session of Stornoway to appoint one further meeting with [the four original appellants] and if within one week of the meeting, they are unprepared to return unconditionally to the regular worship of the congregation, the Kirk Session are authorised to remove

---

[29] The present writer acted as Moderator of the Synod at the point this item was dealt with. Dr John R McIntosh (Aultbea) acted as Clerk.

their names from the Communion Roll." Representatives of the Western Synod dissented from this decision for the following reasons:

> 1. There are clear irregularities in the procedures of the Stornoway Kirk Session.
> 2. There is uncertainty as to the form of censure envisaged as to be imposed on the appellants if they do not cease their current practice.[30]

Though the actions of the men who formed the Stornoway Reformed Fellowship had an appearance of schism, it could be said that the actions to discipline the men were of a dubious nature in formal or pastoral terms. The men themselves denied that they were schismatic but were all too readily disciplined, as indicated in the Synod finding. At any rate this sad incident served to 'up the ante' in the tensions within the Church, something exacerbated in that 1999 General Assembly.

Crisis! – the 1999 General Assembly

Ecclesiastical matters moved with unholy breakneck speed in the course of 1999, leading to the division of January 2000. Though the matter might have seemed to be an internal 'squabble,' in point of fact it was believed that there were serious underlying constitutional issues involved in things as they unfolded in the Church. It was clear that the majority party wished to squeeze out or by sheer votes suppress the 'dissenting elements' represented (as they saw it) by the FCDA.

As it turned out the General Assembly of May 1999 was a watershed. At the outset of one of the Sederunts[31] there was an unseemly and unnecessary questioning by one minister of another who was known to be associated with the FCDA about remarks made in an interview broadcast in a Gaelic radio programme earlier in the morning. During the proceedings the Chairman of the National Committee of the FCDA, the Rev. Maurice Roberts (Inverness), a man whose

---

[30] This was signed by J R McIntosh, Graeme Craig, W Macleod, James I Gracie, R MacKay, John W Keddie. John MacLeod (Tarbat) also dissented with reasons.
[31] The *sederunt* of any Church court refers to those who are present and entitled to take part in the proceedings of the court.

ministry was widely respected within and outside the Free Church, was called on to confirm whether those supportive of the FCDA would contemplate legal action against the Church if it was thought to depart from Free Church principles in any way. Mr Roberts was not able to answer that question decisively because it had not been considered formally in the FCDA. However, in saying during his remarks that he had witnessed some 'irremediable wickedness' in actions of the Assembly there was uproar. The comment was immediately – and wrongly as it happened – understood to refer to the whole Assembly *per se*. He was asked by the Moderator of the Assembly to withdraw what he had said and express sincere regret for it. After a brief recess Mr Roberts asked if in so complex a matter he might be permitted to read a statement. At this point the Principal Clerk intervened to say that "the time for statements is over." Mr Roberts then said that he could not withdraw his remarks because in his heart of hearts he believed what he had said to be true. Consequently, no explanations of Mr Roberts comments were allowed.

The truth is that the Moderator that day was to be blamed in large measure for the train of events set in motion in that situation, because he had the power to curtail it.

(1) In the first place, the Moderator failed to protect the Rev. David Murray (Lochcarron) from what in effect was badgering by the Rev. David Robertson (Dundee) regarding a report on a Gaelic radio programme earlier that day. Mr Robertson felt himself not only to have the right but the responsibility to raise questions about what was allegedly stated by Mr Murray on the radio. However, at that point it was hearsay, and the commissioners of the General Assembly were not fully aware of what had transpired over the airwaves. It seems obvious that the whole matter of what Mr Robertson alleged required to be examined, in fairness to Messrs Murray and Roberts as well as the Church at large. But that required some Committee to examine the matter to enquire whether

potentially censurable things had been said or done in connection with what had been reported on the radio.

(2) In the second place, the Moderator acted bullishly about obtaining a retraction from Mr Roberts of his remark rather than use common sense to quieten the proceedings or ask for an explanation. After all, Mr Roberts' remark about irremediable evil may have sounded unsavoury and may have been ill judged, but it cried out for explanation rather than suppression. Three simple questions arose from Mr Roberts' remarks:

(1) What did he say, exactly?

(2) What did he mean by what he said, precisely?

(3) Was what he said warrantable and supportable?

The mere statement itself, however, was thought to be enough and from that point events in the Church amounted to a stampede towards compulsion or expulsion.[32]

In relation to the claim that he had witnessed 'irremediable wickedness' in the Assembly, Mr Roberts later explained why he made that statement:

> At the close of the debate on the Private Libels it was stated that the 'matter' was 'terminated' forever and must never be reopened in the future. But that is to place a man above the law of the Church. When a matter is terminated it requires first that it be brought to a church trial. This matter has been examined by the Church but has never been the subject of a church trial. The Professor has never been served with a Libel. The verdict of the criminal trial of 1996 does not exempt the Church from carrying out its own trial.
> I call that hypocrisy and wickedness. It attempts to terminate a matter which has greatly troubled the Free Church but it does so in a manner that leaves the problem without remedy. Hence I called it 'irremediable' in my comment from the floor of the Assembly. To act in this way is, surely, "gross" sin.[33]

---

[32] It may be noted that the author personally witnessed these events. For the details of this incident see 'Was it a trap?' in *Free Church Foundations*, July 1999, 14-15.

[33] 'Hypocrisy and Wickedness in the 1999 Assembly,' in *Free Church Foundations*, August 1999, 8-9. The 'Private Libels' in question relates to Libels referred to above in the

It is a sadness that this 'explanation' was never so much as allowed to be heard in any Church court or trial.

The case of Maurice Roberts (June 1999)

One way or another – sadly – division was in the air. Mr Roberts had to be dealt with, and the FCDA had to be suppressed or outlawed. These followed in a series of Commissions of Assembly following the May meeting. Mr Roberts was libelled and judicially suspended *sine die* from the ministry in June.[34] In the course of Mr Roberts' 'trial' it came to light that an audio recording was extant providing what actually had been said at the May Assembly. This confirmed Mr Roberts' own statement that he had not characterised the *whole* Assembly as "irremediably wicked" but that he had witnessed such things in the course of the Assembly. However, this was discounted on the grounds that the Minute had been agreed and Mr Roberts (or others) had had opportunity to correct the minute. In addition to this, in his 'trial' Mr Roberts was prepared to explain what he meant by the statement he made at the Assembly. In the event he was not allowed to make any such explanations on the basis that it was not the detail of what he might have thought to be "irremediably wicked" that was under discussion but simply his refusal to withdraw the remarks when asked (told?) to do so by the Moderator, whatever he might have meant by these remarks! The Assembly of May and the June Commission were not willing to hear arguments that *any* actions of the Assembly were to be characterised as "gross and irremediable wickedness and hypocrisy."

This all hardly amounted to 'transparency' in Church discipline. On the face of it Mr Roberts, as the 'accused', might have been given some leeway in explaining his position and why he felt so strongly about it and in view of an actual audio recording of the original incident the minute might have been altered retrospectively. After all, Church

---

section on *Private Libels raised.*

[34] For details of this issue in the June Commission see (1) *Free Church Foundations*, Special June Commission of Assembly Issue, August 1999, 4-6; and (2) *The Monthly Record*, 'The Commission of Assembly, 23-24 June 1999', August 1999, 179-182.

law is not the law of the Medes and the Persians! The libelling of Mr
Roberts shed no credit either on the moderator of the Assembly or the
Commission charged with dealing with the matter. Subsequently the
FCDA was outlawed in an October Commission. These were both
foolish decisions, involving serious administrative and constitutional
flaws. They were among the actions that were catalysts for division in
the Church.[35]

The Special Commission Report and its outcome (June 1999)[36]

The Special Commission Report was presented to the General
Assembly in May 1999, but through pressure of time consideration of
this was deferred to the Commission of Assembly held on 24th June.
The Commission had received a plethora of diverse submissions from
Church Courts and individuals and the June Commission was faced
with a multiplicity of motions and Overtures arising from the Report
and discussions. The Special Commission itself produced a motion with
6 clauses. For the greater part, the various clauses were somewhat
clichéd or commonplace. The crux lay in the 2nd clause which contained
10 sub-points.

> (1) Affirmations of confessional faithfulness;
> (2) Encouragement to engage in evangelism;
> (3) Reaffirmation of a commitment to Biblical Church
> discipline;
> (4) Recognition of the need for corporate and individual
> repentance;
> (5) A note that no evidence of conspiracy had been brought
> before Church courts;
> (6) A note of regret at the way the media had fuelled the
> matters in dispute;

---

[35] This should be borne in mind before any assumption is made that the division simply
arose out of some irrational unhappiness or disgruntlement over the outcome of the
matter of the allegations involving the College Professor.
[36] See *Minutes of the Proceedings of the Commission of Assembly*, June 1999, 245-256.

(7) A reminder of the mutual respect for ministries in the Free Church notwithstanding a "variety of emphases in ministries within the denomination";

(8) A plea for care in the use of the name 'Free Church';

(9) A statement that whilst recognising freedom of speech it was urged that all throughout the Church should desist from "unhelpful, contentious or divisive polemic" (in the interests of healing divisions);

(10) The Finance, Law and Advisory Committee be directed to reassess the structure and composition of the "Standing Committees, Boards and General Trustees of the Church" in the light of the views of Presbyteries.

Frankly, these motions based on the Report were unlikely to achieve the desired result. There were too many vague and undefined elements. For instance, the claim of a need for corporate and individual repentance was no doubt true enough, though what the nature of the repentance might be, practically speaking, is left unstated. What were people to repent? What was the fault that required repentance? Had it to do with 'conspiracy'? [37] In truth there was a *public fama* concerning a matter of (alleged) conspiracy in that case involving people within the church. 'Conspiracy' seemed to be at the heart both of the Professor's defence and acquittal. Throughout the motions presented there is much said about mutual respect, desisting from divisive polemic, etc., but nothing substantive about righteousness or an appeal to conscience.

In the event the decision of the Commission of June 1999, essentially became a composite from the original motion arising from the Special Commission's Report together with 6 clauses proposed in an Overture from the Presbytery of Edinburgh and Perth. One or two amendments were made to the first motion, notably 2(§9) on 'freedom of speech', the amendment specifying the FCDA being encouraged to early disbandment. Whilst the original motion (even as amended) was somewhat toothless and vague, that could not be said of the 6 clauses

---

[37] See the paragraph, '*The question of a campaign or conspiracy*' in the section, *What were the specific concerns of the FCDA?* in the next chapter.

added arising from the Overture. Office-bearers and members were "instructed" to abide by the 1995 finding and not to pursue that matter "now or henceforth in any form whatsoever" (§1). That smacked of crass authoritarianism. A disagreement, or even what is right or wrong in an issue within a Church, cannot simply be resolved by a majority vote, uncomfortable as that might be.[38] After all, that would just seem another way of asserting the infallibility of the Church! It may be said that this was the most serious departure from the constitution of the Free Church. It meant, essentially, that office bearers and members might be required to 'conceal the truth' and 'remain silent in a just cause.' Furthermore, the Clerk of Assembly was instructed to destroy all the papers in relation to that "matter" forthwith (§2). The Commission was committed not to make comment upon or raise any matter in relation to the proceedings of the Sheriff Court trial (§3) on account of its perception of the "Establishment Principle." This is an astonishing statement which we give in full here:

> The Commission of Assembly, acknowledging that the Free Church of Scotland holds to the Establishment Principle and accepts "the magistrate's just and legal authority…from which ecclesiastical persons are not excepted" (*Confession of Faith*, chap. XXIII, para. iv), recognise that the proceedings of the 1996 Sheriff Court case concluding in the acquittal of Professor Donald Macleod are, like the proceedings of any state court, under the sole jurisdiction of the State, and that the Church has no further jurisdiction in those proceedings. Wherefore, the Commission of Assembly resolve not to

---

[38] It may be said that when issues arise in Church courts votes will be taken and the majority vote will carry the day. This is accepted practice and usually passes without dissent. Dissents, simple or with reasons, or protests, when feelings on an issue are sufficiently strong, have often been lodged readily enough without much incident (albeit often with answers to any reasons given for dissents or protests). However, majority votes should never be an oppressive or suppressive instrument when there are differences conscientiously held on what are seen to be important matters for the Church (within its constitution). In that case continuing moves for correction or redress must be lived with, however uncomfortable to the 'peace' of the Church. Dispeace should never just be put down to a dissenting minority. Frequently, agreed matters that are retrospectively seen to be wrong are later repealed, often arising from agitation to do so from within the Church (whether by erstwhile protesters or otherwise).

comment upon or raise any matter in connection with the
proceedings of the said Sheriff Court Trial.

The Church, however, is not bound to be uncritical of decisions of civil
or criminal courts if they consider them to be a miscarriage of justice.
Consider the Veto Act of 1834. This Act gave parishioners the right to
reject a minister nominated by their patron. Yet that flew in the face of
the law of the land in the form of the Patronage Act of 1712. Or take
the whole thrust of the *Claim of Right* of 1842, rejected by Parliament
early in 1843. This was a contributory cause of the Disruption that May.
A Commission of Assembly may choose not to comment upon or raise
matters relating to any State legislation or Court judgments, but that has
nothing to do with the 'Establishment Principle' or respect for the
authority of the powers that be. On the basis of the arguments here the
Church of Scotland or the Free Church of Scotland might have made
no comment or criticism of the workings of the Patronage Act, or the
1967 Abortion Act for that matter, or more recent legislation on same-
sex marriage!   In any case, does the Church not have a duty of pastoral
care, or for that matter disciplinary action, in connection with members
or ministers *maligned* or accused of wrongdoing (perjury?) in such a
court action? The matter is not resolved simply by invoking the
establishment principle without regard to what is *righteous*. After all, it is
at the very least *possible* that a Sheriff Court verdict is *not* righteous,
something, indeed, which was not unreasonably argued by many in
relation to the case in 1996.

Other addenda were more fearful and threatening and were
quite a contrast to a Special Commission supposedly set on 'peace and
reconciliation': Church courts which received information of any
members or office-bearers of the Free Church who did not comply
with the instruction (not to pursue the matter in any form whatsoever)
should, essentially, have disciplinary action taken against them (§4).
Office-bearers and members of the Free Church are "instructed" to
cease "canvassing outwith the Church matters properly dealt with by
church courts." There was also a warning about church courts hearing
of any individual under its jurisdiction not complying with this

instruction being required to instigate disciplinary action against them (§5). All ministers in pastoral charges were instructed to intimate the findings (of §1 to §5, which became clauses 7 to 11 of the final finding) by public intimation before 31ˢᵗ July 1999 (§6).

Protest

In the event dissent and protest was tabled against this final finding in the following terms:

> Furthermore, we subscribers, for ourselves, and on behalf of others who may adhere, do protest against the resolution to adopt as an addendum to the Report of the Special Commission the substance of the Overture from the Presbytery of Edinburgh and Perth, now adopted by this Commission, and that on the following, among other grounds:
> 1ˢᵗ. Because the resolution, as adopted, implies an abandonment and subversion of a constitutional principle of the Free Church of Scotland and is contrary to the *Form of Process*.
> 2ⁿᵈ. Because the resolution, as adopted, is *ultra vires* of this Commission.
> For these and other reasons, we protest, that we and all other office-bearers and members of the Church shall not be committed to [by?] the said resolution to any action that may be taken thereupon, and shall be at liberty to oppose all such action by every competent means.[39]

It can be well understood just how much of a farce the *Addendum* made of the "Special Commission to seek Reconciliation"! It was in effect a gagging order imposed on the minority section on issues in dispute. What had been intended as a 'peace accord' had essentially become an instrument of oppression! Its application would depend on 'votes.'

---

[39] *Minutes of the Proceedings of the Commission of* Assembly, June, 1999, 255-256. This dissent and protest was subscribed by John MacLeod (Tarbat), W. Macleod, James I Gracie, John J Harding, John A Gillies, P B Matheson, Roderick McKay, A MacKenzie, A N Nicolson, Fraser Couper, and Alasdair Morrison

In the next chapter we shall deal with the specific events from which the unhappy division occurred in the Free Church and out of which the Free Church of Scotland (Continuing) emerged in 2000.

FREE CHURCH DEFENCE ASSOCIATION
ACTED AGAINST, 1999

Division occurred in the Free Church of Scotland on 20th January 2000. This arose directly from the unprecedented libelling of 32 ministers by the determination of the Commission of Assembly that met in December 1999.[1] How exactly did this division occur? Was the libelling of so many ministers, something unprecedented in Scottish Presbyterian history, really justified? We begin by looking at the *bête noir* of the majority – the Free Church Defence Association. This Association was at the heart of the displeasure of the Free Church, as represented by the majority of the members of the General Assembly in May 1999.

What was the Free Church Defence Association?

The Free Church Defence Association was re-formed in 1997. To make clear its platform, the re-formed Association stated its position to be the same as that of the Association established in 1870. The *principles* were rooted in the Free Church testimony enshrined in the *Claim of Right* (1842), the Protest and *Deed of Demission* (1843) and the *Formula* of 1846. These things were still affirmed by the Free Church in 1997. As an Association it could hardly be said to be 'divisive' in principles. But what about its *Aims*? In 1997 these were clearly stated:

1. To defend, maintain and promote the Biblical and Confessional doctrines and practice of the historic Free Church of Scotland.

---

[1] Of the 32 one withdrew his name before the Commission of December 1999 and one was withdrawn by the Church on account of serious illness, though he had not requested such action. The minister who withdrew his name subsequently entered the Free Presbyterian Church.

2. To defend and promote the regulative principle in Divine worship and to resist innovations in worship not sanctioned by the Word of God.

3. To uphold and defend the Presbyterian church government and discipline of the Free Church.

4. To press for consistency and adherence to ordination vows on the part of ministers, professors and office-bearers of the Free Church.

5. To promote, through publications, meetings and otherwise, the historic principles of the Free Church and to inform the people of the Church of matters bearing on these principles.

6. To promote and encourage godliness in conduct.

7. To promote peace, unity and brotherly love on the basis of Biblical truth and righteousness.

Far from any true-hearted Free Church person being alarmed at such an Association with such principles and aims, it might be thought it would inspire admiration and be lauded by any who were committed to the Free Church doctrine, worship, government and practice. There was no way that the principles of this Association *as such* could have been characterised as divisive. In the event it appears that clause 5 in the 'Aims' became, in essence, the contentious point within the Church.

The majority party, however, in the Free Church of 1999 in an authoritarian judgment maintained that the *actions* of the FCDA were censurable. On 7th October 1999, the Commission of Assembly of the Free Church declared, arbitrarily, that "the Free Church Defence Association is pursuing a divisive course from the government and discipline of the Free Church of Scotland." This 'third party' organisation therefore became a 'soft target' for those who disliked the concerns being raised by those associated with the FCDA. That, however, was one of the perversities and questionable constitutional actions of the majority in the Commissions of Assembly in the last quarter of 1999 and in January 2000.

What were the specific concerns of the FCDA?

1. The question of a campaign or conspiracy

Those who were sympathetic with the principles and aims of the FCDA were concerned over what they saw as a lack of real discipline in the Church. Notwithstanding the Sheriff Court decision of 1996, it was maintained that the Church was duty-bound to come to its own decision in such matters, and there was sufficient concern over the inadequacy of the prosecution in the case as to leave a question open about the justice of the decision. In addition, the supporters of the FCDA felt that in any case the Professor's defence of 'conspiracy' required to be examined in the Church, either for the discipline of conspirators or their vindication as non-conspirators. A Church is responsible under Christ for righteousness to be done and to be seen to be done. At various points before, during, and after the trial in the Sheriff Court different expressions were used to describe how the case against the Professor had arisen.

The Professor himself at that time was inclined to use the term 'campaign.' It was reported in *The Scotsman* at the time of the case that "Macleod claims to be the victim of a campaign," this with reference to the thrust of his defence. It was reported: "Macleod said he did not think there was a conspiracy against him. 'I do not like the word…It implies overtness and covertness. This is a campaign'."[2] It is fair to ask what the difference is. Either way this was a serious allegation. But in fact after the first Commission of Assembly on 2nd October, 1996, he wrote explicitly "I categorically reject the idea there was no conspiracy. That conspiracy had its crowning triumph in Edinburgh on Wednesday when the conspirators showed a level of organisation, ruthlessness and cunning which the goodness in the Church simply cannot match."[3]

It was with some perceptiveness and reality that Iain Murray observed that "if the action of some men at that time began to assume the aspect of a campaign, it is no less true that *another* campaign was

[2] *The Scotsman*, Tuesday, 18 June 1996.
[3] *West Highland Free Press*, 11 October 1996.

already operating on behalf of Professor Macleod, and this was a campaign within the Free Church to have all allegations against him dismissed."[4] This view seems to be justified when account is taken of a Memorial in support of the Professor issued as early as May 1995. This Memorial, which craved that the matter be concluded without delay, was sent on to the Principal Clerk. It was signed by 65 ministers, 155 elders, 72 deacons, 840 members and 343 adherents. This surely was indicative of a 'campaign' every bit as much, if not more so, than any actions of those *unhappy* with the way the allegations/complaints against the Professor had been handled in the Church!

This of course might be disputed. But what is not disputed is that with the emergence of *Free Concern* immediately following the first Commission of October 1996, there was clearly by then – before the FCDA came on to the scene – a degree of organisation in 'defence' of the Professor. The issuing of a Petition in that connection from an 'organised' meeting after that Commission, had a distinctly polarising influence in the Church, especially where signatures in support of it were solicited in local congregations. By any measure the whole matter of 'campaign' or 'conspiracy,' one way or another, impinged upon the reputation of the Church. That was a concern for the FCDA.

2. *Other issues of concern*

Besides concerns arising from the allegations of misconduct on the part of the Professor in question and the action in the courts of the land against him, as well as actions – or inactions – with the Church, there were concerns too about statements made by him in the press and media that on the face of it flew in the face of ministerial ordination vows. Indeed, some of these concerns had come to the Church from another Reformed Church in 1997.

---

[4] Iain H Murray, *Professor Donald Macleod and His 'Opponents'*, London, 1996, 15. As already indicated, it could be maintained that at an earlier stage (even as early as 1987) there was some evidence of a 'campaign' to avoid any formal enquiry into moral allegations involving the said Professor.

In a communication from the Reformed Presbyterian Church of Ireland arising from their Synod of June 1997 concerns were expressed over various statements attributable to the said Professor. They picked up, firstly, on a transcript of an Interview on BBC Radio Scotland on 30th June 1996: "My concern is to go back to Jesus. I even feel uncomfortable going back to St. Paul. I think the Church has lost contact with Galilee to a very large extent. The instinct I want to develop is to ask 'what would Jesus do in the circumstances?' And so much discussion in the Church for the last 2000 years has been, in my view, quite unconnected with Jesus. We don't ask His type of questions and if we were to ask Him our questions He would just smile benignly I think and shake His head in disbelief at what interests us." "Here," says the RPCI letter, "Professor Macleod draws a distinction between the teachings of our Lord as recorded in the gospels and the writings of the Apostle Paul, which appears to place the two on different levels of importance and authority. On the basis of Scripture we believe that both have equal authority and importance when they are recorded in the inspired scriptures. 1 Corinthians 11:23; 1 Thessalonians 2:13; 2 Peter 3:16. Such a disjunction appears to give reverence to the person of our Lord, but is in fact the position of much nineteenth century liberalism, which led to the widespread denial of many of our Lord's teachings."

Among other things, the RPCI letter also highlighted a statement made by Donald Macleod in the *West Highland Free Press* on 29 December, 1995: "The other thing that is so impressive is the risk that Jesus took: the risk that the Cross would be the End and that He would never come back." On this point the comment is well made: "We reject the idea that our Lord took a risk when He offered Himself as a sacrifice for our sins on the cross. This is contrary to the teaching of scripture and the Confession of Faith. Our Lord died to make the salvation of the elect certain. He went to the cross on the basis of God's eternal decree. 'God from all eternity did, by the most wise and holy counsel of His own will, freely and unchangeably ordain

whatsoever comes to pass' (WCF 3.1). As the Son of God He knew
what would come to pass, because it had already been decreed, and He
knew that God's decrees, rather than change, govern the universe."[5]
The majority, however, were in no mind even to investigate such things.
In a somewhat docile way the Assembly accepted 'explanations' via one
of her most senior ministers.[6]

The FCDA felt that there was weakness also in the area of
purity of worship, as well as theological matters such as those
highlighted by the Reformed Presbyterians, which carried some weight
coming as they did from outside the Church. In addition, on occasion
the Professor made liberal-sounding statements, as for example about
legalising cannabis use.[7] However fair or unfair the reporting may have
been, all these matters involved directly attributable statements within
the public domain. Thus, they were legitimate concerns of the men
associated with the FCDA, or for that matter any other interested
parties and the Church at large.

Another area of concern related to purity of worship. There
seemed to be a distinct weakening of attachment in parts of the Church
to purity of worship. For example, it was reported at the end of 1997
that there was a 'Carol Service' held in the Free Church in Aberdeen,
with hymns and instrumental music. On this issue the General
Assembly accepted the essence of an Overture from the Presbytery of

---

[5] See the full text of this letter in *Free Church Foundations*, October, 1997.

[6] The 1998 Assembly contained a strong representation of those sympathetic to the
FCDA. The fact that concerns regarding the Professor raised by the RPCI were not
pursued in that Assembly very likely arose from a focus on other issues arising in that
Assembly and a lack of specific preparation in connection with an item that arose from
outwith the Free Church. However, on 13th June 2001 the RPCI came to the following
finding: "Because of the apparent unwillingness or inability of the Free Church of
Scotland to take the necessary disciplinary action against Rev. Prof. Donald Macleod we
suspend fraternal relationship with that body. In view of our long and close relationship
with the Free Church of Scotland this decision is taken with the utmost regret."

[7] See the cartoon by Ian White in *The Scotsman* in 1999 (20th August), depicting someone
at the Professor's door in the Free Church College and hearing the invitation: "Come
away in – you'll have had your joint." In the *Metro* of Monday, October 23, 2000, there
was a piece entitled 'Make cannabis legal, says Wee Free leader' (with reference to
Professor Macleod's reported views).

Lewis which clearly re-affirmed the purity of worship as presently practised in the Free Church.

The FCDA is acted against

The crux of the matter occurred at the October Commission of 1999. Finally, there was a move against the FCDA. The fact of an FCDA might not have been liked, but really the organisation itself was unexceptional, and though thought to be 'troublesome' by the movements for change in the 19th century Free Church, there was never any question of acting against men because of their association with it, notwithstanding the fact that the Association then also had magazines producing materials very critical of the pro-union party, General Assembly decisions and the like.

In 1999, however, an Overture to the Commission of Assembly on 7th October 1999 from the Presbytery of Lewis was radical. Its 'crave' became the finding of the Commission, namely:

1. They declare that the Free Church Defence Association is pursuing a divisive course from the government and discipline of the Free Church of Scotland;
2. They declare that the office-bearers of the FCDA have adopted a position that is in violation of their position as office-bearers of the Free Church of Scotland;
3. They call upon the FCDA to disband immediately, requesting that they give notice of their having disbanded to the Principal Clerk by 30th November 1999 at the latest, failing which,
4. The Commission of Assembly instruct all Presbyteries to,
   (i) Inform all office-bearers – ministers, elders and deacons of the Free Church of Scotland – within their bounds who wish to hold office both in the Free Church of Scotland and in the Free Church Defence Association that they are thereby in breach of their ordination vows; and
   (ii) Require all office-bearers of the Free Church of Scotland within their bounds who are also office-bearers of the Free

Church Defence Association that they will forthwith resign their office in the Free Church Defence Association, or else be liable to be declared contumacious[8] in that they will thereby have expressed a resolve to continue their pursuit of an unlawful and unbiblical course of action; in which case Presbyteries are instructed to initiate proceedings against any office-bearer of the Free Church of Scotland who declares that he will not resign his office in the Free Church Defence Association.

So, what objections were and are there to such findings?

Objections to the anti-FCDA Finding

1. First of all there is the point that *it was declarative*. It merely declared that the FCDA was pursuing a divisive course, though it did not state in what respects that was the case, except in the vague and unspecific "from the government and discipline of the Free Church of Scotland." The idea was that simply by declaring the FCDA to be divisive it was also *ipso facto* declaring any individuals who were members of the FCDA to be divisive, though previously it had been stated that the FCDA had no locus in the courts of the Church. The most that could be said about an Association like the FCDA is that its position, in terms of principles and aims, was at variance with the doctrine or processes of the Church. However, that would require to be demonstrated. But that could not be done in the case of the FCDA as such. There was patently nothing in the stated principles and aims of the FCDA that provided the least grounds for such a claim.

2. Secondly, there was a declaration that office-bearers in the FCDA *were automatically in violation of ordination vows* merely by association with

---

[8] *Contumacy* in church law is stubbornness, obstinacy or perversity. In this case it was defiance of what was considered a legitimate instruction. It became, as it turned out, the favoured way of dealing with the 'troublesome' FCDA by a majority of the votes in the Commissions of Assembly that year. If there was 'obstinacy' it was by no means all on one side. It was a matter of votes. There was 'perversity,' it may be argued, with the manipulators of the contumacy idea!

the FCDA. How could they be in violation of their ordination vows? To what does their ordination vow bind them? Basically, they are obliged to disown all "Popish, Arian, Socinian, Arminian, Erastian, and other doctrines, tenets and opinions whatsoever, contrary to, or inconsistent with, the foresaid Confession of Faith."[9] To act against men for mere association with the FCDA, against which there was only an unspecific claim that it was following a divisive course from the government and discipline of the Church, was in fact a violation *on the part of the Church* in relation to the ordination vows of its ministers. How was that the case? Because it was in effect arbitrarily altering the vows to include a proscribed Association without first going through the process of incorporating such a proscription in the vows via due ecclesiastical processes. In that respect it was in effect a constructive denial of a *right to protest* on the part of ministers who genuinely felt that things were being approved of in the Church at odds with their own ordination vows!

It is true that the minister (or elder) is also obliged to submit "willingly and humbly, in the spirit of meekness, unto the admonitions of the brethren" of Presbytery or higher courts and to "follow no divisive course from the doctrine, worship, discipline, and government of this Church."[10] That, however, is not 'open-ended,' but is within the context of the commitment of the office-bearers to the biblical and constitutional position of the Church. It would remain to be proven that actions of ministers and elders did show deviation from the doctrine, worship, government or discipline of the Church. In that connection it cannot possibly be self-evident that they are thus guilty simply because the majority of a Commission or Assembly declare that some Christian Association or other has been following a divisive course without specifically stating that the individuals were involved in that alleged divisiveness and that such an alleged divisiveness was clearly contrary to the teaching of Scripture!

---

[9] *The Practice of the Free Church of Scotland in Her Several Courts*, Edinburgh, [8]1995, 152.
[10] ibid., 153.

3. In the third place there are also serious objections to the *instruction to the Presbyteries* as to what they would be required to do in the event of the office-bearers within their bounds failing to comply with the instruction to disband the FCDA and disassociate with it:

1. *It was improper to state to Presbyteries that those who remained in the FCDA were in breach of their ordination vows.* That begged the question. In what respect were they in breach of their ordination vows? If it was being associated with the FCDA, that could not be a breach, in itself, of ordination vows, as the FCDA are not mentioned in the ordination vows. Was it because the FCDA was declared to be following a 'divisive course' and all associated with it as office-holders must *ipso facto* be following a divisive course? That is all very well, but the finding that the FCDA was following a divisive course did not specify in what respects or provide proof of what ways it was following such a course. It is true that the Church's office bearers ought to give all due respect to decisions of Assemblies and Commissions. According to the finding of October 7th, however, it was defiance of the General Assembly (or its Commissions) that was the basis of the breach of ordination vows, simply in continuing to hold office in the FCDA against the arbitrary declarative finding of the Commission of Assembly. In any case all decisions or instructions or requirements by higher courts themselves require to be both biblical and agreeable to established Church law. Can a man really be in breach of ordination vows simply because the majority of an Assembly or Commission declares that a body with which he is an office-holder, not named in the ordination vows, is reckoned by that majority to be divisive, without specificity? In truth that was cross authoritarianism in Church law, an unwarranted *magisterial* action.

2. Furthermore, *it was improper to mention the nature of the guilt before there had even been a case in which the individual whom the Presbytery*

was to say was in breach of ordination vows had any opportunity to defend himself! This is what the finding states: "liable to be declared contumacious." That is prejudicing the case. It was saying, in effect: 'These men are to be disciplined, and when they are, this is what they will be found guilty of!' It certainly appears that this was designed to ensure that the Presbyteries came to the right conclusion according to the view of a majority of the Commission as then constituted. The individuals disciplined, presumably, could not even ask the question: "How is the FCDA following a 'divisive course,' please specify and I will defend the FCDA against such a claim?" But that could not happen because the Presbyteries had to accept the diktat that the FCDA was guilty of following a divisive course!

3. *There was misapplication of the disciplinary process.* This whole scenario was a scandalous mal-application of proper disciplinary process. It was what might be called an 'entrapment policy,' using the soft target of a 'third party,' which, in itself, in terms of its basis and aims, was unexceptional and even admirable. In effect, the process was *inviting* contumacy because it is hard to see how men who were *not* convinced that the FCDA was following a divisive course would disassociate from it, especially since the purported divisiveness was neither specified nor proved! Being declarative it also ran the serious risk of simply infringing the constitutional rights of the Church's office-bearers by, in effect, *adding* to their vows (contract with the Church) something *additional* to what was specifically in the vows, without clear biblical grounds or constitutional process.[11]

---

[11] The argument has been made that 'declarative' statements in Church legislation implementing a policy or law in the Church should automatically be passed down to the Presbyteries for approval under Barrier Act legislation. It can therefore be argued that constitutionally this is a seriously missing element in the whole procedure in this case. See J K Cameron, *The Clerkship of the General Assembly of the Free Church of Scotland,* Inverness, 1938, 93-4.

4. *Was the FCDA really guilty of an "unlawful and unbiblical course of action"?* This is averred in the 'finding,' though notably it is not demonstrated by biblical arguments. It seemed to be simply a pious-sounding phrase taken for granted rather than proved. Yet it is a 'crux.' Where does righteousness fit into the picture here? On the face of it all the FCDA concerns were 'righteous.' The question might well be asked: Could the majority be found to be acting without biblical substance? It is not a biblical principle that because the majority in a Church feels a thing to be wrong it is therefore beyond challenge.

This is not to say that office-bearers in the FCDA may not have been guilty of following a divisive course from the government and discipline of the Church. But that was a matter with which the individuals in question were never individually confronted. Instead they were confronted with something against which they had no real defence, at least if they considered the Church to be unsound and unwarranted in characterising the FCDA as divisive. The finding itself for reasons stated was constitutionally unsound because it was based on an unsubstantiated declaration or declarations. Nothing might have come from this finding. The question was: what would the FCDA office-bearers do?

The FCDA response

On 29th November 1999 a communication was sent from the National Committee of the FCDA intimating that in the present circumstances disbandment was not considered an appropriate course of action. In the document it was stated that, "Notwithstanding our due respect to the superior judicatories of the Free Church of Scotland, and the Commission of Assembly in particular, and our wholehearted determination to obey all lawful demands laid on us by the said judicatories when acting in accordance with the constitution of the Free Church of Scotland,

1. We repudiate any suggestion 'that the FCDA is following a divisive course from the government and discipline of the Free Church of Scotland.'
2. We repudiate any suggestion 'that the Officebearers of the FCDA have adopted a position that is in violation of their position as Officebearers of the Free Church of Scotland.'
3. We believe we are duty bound by solemn ordination vows both to God and the Free Church of Scotland to uphold the constitution of the historic Free Church of Scotland and it is to that end that we are resolved to continue the FCDA in existence in view of the present concerns felt about numerous actions and perceived injustices imposed by the majority party in this year's Assembly and Commissions as well as other recent Findings of Assemblies and its Commission which we believe are *ultra vires* and injurious of the peace, well-being and good name of the Free Church of Scotland.
4. We, furthermore, affirm our support for Rev William Macleod, Editor, and Rev David P. Murray, Assistant Editor, of *Free Church Foundations* and confirm that it is the National Committee of the FCDA which is responsible for publishing *Free Church Foundations* Magazine, not the Editors."

This statement was signed by 32 ministers, including 18 in charges. Of the signatories two were past Moderators of the General Assembly and several had been Conveners of standing Committees in the Church, and one was in his 90th year with over 50 years of service as a minister of the Church! The reason for such a positive support was the conviction on the one hand of the flawed declarative finding of the October 1999 Commission of Assembly, and the conviction that the Commission had overstepped the bounds of its authority. There was also a desire to support the Editors of the FCDA magazines who had been threatened with disciplinary action. This was thought to be not at all fair given that there were many contributors of (unattributed) articles that had appeared in *Free Church Foundations*.

DIVISION IN THE FREE CHURCH
1999-2000

The response of the Free Church Defence Association in November 1999 was clearly a crux. On the face of it their points were made courteously and reasonably. But how would the Commission appointed for December react? Questions arose: How could a division in the Church be avoided? Who would be responsible for it? Answers to these questions are not as straightforward as they might appear to be, as we shall see.

The December Commission, 1999

Whether the majority who had supported the findings of the October Commission expected this, the Commissioners who gathered in Edinburgh for another Commission appointed for 8th December were faced with a challenging situation. The powers of a Commission are severely limited and scarcely give it authority to act as judge, jury and dispensers of ecclesiastical punishments in the light of the *Form of Process* (1707).[1] But would it embark upon a disciplinary process against 32 ministers whose ecclesiastical crime was to be office-bearers in the FCDA, an Association proscribed without any change to the ordination position of the ministers? This is an interesting question.

In the event the Commission considered that the FCDA statement providing grounds for refusing to disband the Association was presented "under the cloak of submission to the judicatories of the Church," and furthermore on the face of it represented an "act of continued and wilful contumacy." The Commission also assumed to itself the inherent authority of dealing with the matter *instanter*.[2] A Committee, under the convenership of the Rev. Alex MacDonald

---

[1] *Practice*, 180ff.
[2] That is to say, 'immediately' (i.e., no delay).

(Buccleuch and Greyfriars, Edinburgh) was appointed to draft and prosecute libels against the 32 ministers in question, such libels to be dealt with at yet another meeting of Commission, on 19th January 2000.

Never in the history of the Presbyterian Church in Scotland had anything like this been undertaken.[3] It had all the appearance of what it was: a serious abuse of disciplinary process. Despite this, the Free Church, post-2000, by and large seemed to escape the disapproval of other Christian bodies and for the greater part enjoyed the favour of the press, over against the minority who were sometimes – unfairly – described as 'hardliners.' Was the majority party not the 'hard-line' faction in this instance? No doubt it depends on one's standpoint. The libelled ministers, therefore, faced an unsavoury and stressful situation, though there was little they could do, since the charge would be 'contumacy'[4] which if found 'relevant' would basically be unchallengeable. The Roberts' case had apparently provided the *modus operandi* at Church law by which to 'excise the boil' of a troublesome minority. In truth it was crass authoritarianism in Church procedures.

Procedural and Constitutional Issues [5]
Serious questions arose in the procedures adopted in the Commissions of Assembly held between June 1999 and January 2000 when 30 ministers[6] were cited to appear to answer libels served on them, namely, the charge of continued contumacious behaviour:

---

[3] In different circumstances, in 1663 270 Presbyterian ministers were removed from their Parishes in Scotland under an Act of Parliament after the restoration of Charles II. See J H S Burleigh, *A Church History of Scotland*, London, 1960, 245-6. The mass libelling of ministers in the Free Church in 2000 is, however, without parallel as a matter of discipline within the Scottish Presbyterian Church.
[4] *Contumacy* in Church law is the ignoring or denying or resisting what is considered as a perfectly lawful requirement or instruction of a Church Court.
[5] For this section the writer is indebted to the comments of Maurice Grant (elder, Free St Columba's Edinburgh) which he put in a paper to help prepare ministers in addressing their libels in January 2000.
[6] This included one minister in his 90th year and eight ministers each of whom had served in the ministry for over 30 years. See Appendix 1.

1. Was the process according to proper Presbyterian order?

It is exceptional for a General Assembly – or any Commission of Assembly – to be a court of first instance in disciplinary matters. A matter would have to be forced on its attention before it has reached an inferior court (where such actions normally start). In such a case the Assembly may refer the matter to the inferior court, which has jurisdiction over the individual, or deal with it summarily.[7] It would appear to be the responsibility of General Assemblies to preserve the rights of Presbyteries, according to the *Form of Process*: "all processes against any minister are to begin before the Presbytery to which he belongeth."[8] There was a case in 1838 in which a commissioner to an Assembly (i.e. Church of Scotland) was seen to be intoxicated at the Assembly Hall and also in the streets of the city. The Assembly appointed a committee to enquire of the situation and summoned the minister to the bar. However, the Assembly refrained from libelling him itself but sent the precognitions to the said minister's Presbytery with instructions to libel him and report the outcome to the Commission.[9] Such a procedure was in line with the *Form of Process*, though neither in the case of the Rev. Maurice Roberts in May 1999, nor the 30 ministers libelled in December 1999, was there recourse to any Presbytery for pursuit of the libels.

Naturally, because of the approach via the purported divisiveness of the FCDA, and in view of the fact that so many ministers were involved, it was preferable, if constitutionally questionable, to deal with all the men *without* going to the Presbyteries, given that Presbyteries might have arrived at different judgements! Unlike the case of Maurice Roberts in which the alleged offence was committed *in facie ecclesiae*,[10] the purported 'offences' of the FCDA

---

[7] *Practice*, 113-114.
[8] ibid., 191.
[9] This was the case of Donald Maclean, Small Isles, within the Presbytery of Skye. It was dealt with in the General Assembly, 26th and 28th May 1838, and the Commission of Assembly, 21st November 1838. Mr Maclean was deposed from the ministry consequent upon the proof of the libel against him.

office-bearers were *not* forced upon the attention of the Church Courts by being committed in the actual presence of the Courts.

It was argued that there was precedent for treating a purportedly contumacious statement in writing as on a par with it being actually made in the face of the Court. However, that tended to be the recourse of Moderates. For example, in 1733 when Ebenezer Erskine tabled a protest against a rebuke he received in the Assembly, the protest was found to be contumacious by the Assembly. Erskine and three others were ordered to appear before the next Commission and, if they refused to withdraw the protest, they would be suspended from the ministry. One historian of the Secession Church wrote of that situation:

> The very forms of justice were disregarded, in the present instance, by those haughty ecclesiastics. For respect even to the shadow and letter of justice, should evidently dispose those who sit in judgment, to allow the utmost latitude of defence to those who are cited before them, and whose interests are deeply involved in the decision. This is one of those forms which no circumstance should be allowed to violate, and which having their foundation in natural justice, have often proved the invaluable safeguards of human rights. What shall we think then of such a decision summarily passed against these four brethren, while all inquiry is foreclosed and defence interdicted. Hasty decisions are a sure indication that faction or fear is sitting as judge. How true is the remark of Milton that, from the foundation of the world, error has never dared an open encounter with truth, or tyranny with an honest cause.[11]

---

[10] This is a Latin term which means "in the face or presence of the church." It is used in English law to apply to marriages solemnized in a parish church or public chapel. The term itself does not appear in the *Practice*, nor in Robert Forbes' 19th century Free Church *Digest of Rules and Procedures*. It seems to have been used in the 1999 General Assembly by the Principal Clerk to provide some *gravitas* to the course of events involving Mr Roberts, although the alleged 'offense' was not actually what he said but his refusal to withdraw remarks he was not given latitude to explain!

[11] Andrew Thomson, *Historical Sketch of the Origin of the Secession Church*, Edinburgh, 1848, 60-61.

"Tyranny with an honest cause." If ever there was a remark applicable to the unseemly proceedings of the Commissions in the Free Church of 1999/2000 then that was the remark! The majority, of course, would be horrified to think their actions might be likened to "tyranny" or the ignominious actions of the Moderates in the Established Church in 1733. Nevertheless, in this instance that was a logical implication of their actions and decisions!

2. What authority does a Commission of Assembly really have?
The status and powers of the Commission of Assembly seemed to be misunderstood, not to say exaggerated. It can be argued that the Commission of an Assembly is *not* a court of the church at all! Former Principal Clerk of the Assembly, Rev. William Macleod (Dornoch), wrote in the *Monthly Record* of August 1950 about the status of Commissions in this vein: "There is no indication that the Commission of Assembly – ordinary or special – is anything other than 'A Commission to certain ministers and elders for discussing affairs referred to them' [Act I, 1844] and to invest it with the status of a church court is unconstitutional and a dangerous intrusion upon the Presbyterian order."[12] According to the *Practice* it can only deal with cases to the extent that these are specifically referred to it by the Assembly.[13] Furthermore, it can determine private processes only at one of the *stated* diets (March/October). The diets of December 1999 and January 2000 did not fall into that category.

There is a clause which states that a Commission requires to "advert to the interests of the church on every occasion, that the church do not suffer or sustain any prejudice which they can prevent, as they will be answerable." This was pressed into use in the 1999/2000 period. But really, to stretch the meaning of that clause to adopt almost unlimited powers in raising libels (without reference to Presbyteries or remit from an Assembly), and pronounce suspensions, must be seriously questioned. It was apparently believed that decisive action was

---

[12] *The Monthly Record of the Free Church of Scotland*, August 1950, 162-163.
[13] *Practice*, 86-87.

necessary "in order to prevent major breakdown throughout the whole denomination."[14] That, however, was a speculative point and the subsequent action taken was simply related to personal opinions and weight of votes. It may be suggested that the majority might rather have followed the advice of Gamaliel: "keep away from these men and let them alone; for if this plan or this work is of men, it will come to nothing; but if it is of God, you cannot overthrow it, lest you even be found to fight against God" (Acts 5:38-39).

The fact is that the procedures adopted in the June 1999 to January 2000 period can be interpreted as a shameful misapplication or 'twisting' of the disciplinary process. In December 1995 the Commission was invited by the Training of the Ministry Committee to instruct a Professor to cease immediately from the discharge of his duties pending the outcome of criminal proceedings. In that case the Commission rejected such a request as *ultra vires* the powers of the Commission. In 1999, however, the Commission was deemed so powerful that it could libel 30 ministers at will without any remit from the General Assembly and without going near a Presbytery! By any measure it was a disgrace in the (*ultra vires*) Church's administration of discipline.

3. *Was 'contumacy' a reasonable and fair charge?*

The charge of contumacy as used in the 1999/2000 period in the Free Church was effectively a means of manipulation of an offence that had varied applications according to circumstances. Normally it is applied when the subjects of an alleged offence fail to respond to citations to appear to give an account of themselves and the alleged misdemeanour. The circumstances of the libels against the 30 ministers in December 1999/January 2000 gave the impression that the majority had been looking for a means by which they might avoid awkward questions and issues and defences being adopted. Having effectively proscribed the FCDA and made office in it incompatible with office in the Free

[14] See the article 'What was the Secession about?', in *The Monthly Record*, March 2000, 54-55.

Church, the possibility was opened up of a charge in which *no issues would be raised or discussed.* It is only fair to state that the actions of the majority were also motivated by the hope that the brethren associated with the FCDA would back down or relinquish office in the FCDA. That, however, was an *oppressive* motive by a majority upon a minority, and a rather disingenuous ploy to 'gag' a section of the Church from pursuing what were considered troublesome issues, without assessing their righteousness. So, contumacy was the answer! Was this a fair charge? We think not. Rather, if there was a suspicion that men were following a divisive course, then that matter should have been raised in Presbyteries on an individual basis with 'divisive course' as the charge or accusation.

One of the interesting issues in this case lay in the fact that 8 men did not appear before the Commission of Assembly in January 2000, six of whom presented medical certificates or letters providing reasons for absence. What happened to these six men subsequently? In fact, no formal action was taken. They were excused from further processes ostensibly on 'compassionate' grounds. However, if the offence was so great as to justify possible deposition,[15] even a medical certificate is surely no immunity from such disciplinary action. If six could be so readily excused, why not the others? The impression is given that it was all simply a means of wholesale suppression, and if necessary, deposition.

The Free Church issued a *Statement to other Churches* about this purported disciplinary action on 28th January 2000. This stated, among other things:

> We wish to assure everyone that when this secession took place we were carrying out disciplinary procedures in accordance with our constitution and in faithfulness to the Scriptures and the Confession of Faith...The charge which these ministers faced was contumacy, that is, defiance of the

---

[15] In the Libels issued in December 1999 it was stated that "and if the facts be proved to the satisfaction of the said Commission of Assembly, you will be liable to such censure, *not excluding deposition from the Ministry*, as may to the said Commission seem appropriate" (*italics* mine – JWK).

> Presbyterian courts of this Church by following a divisive
> course from the government and discipline of the Church...

The residuary Free Church[16] apparently was unaware of a significant admission in this statement. The office bearers of the FCDA were, it says, charged with contumacy *by following a divisive course from the government and discipline of the Church*. But you can't have it both ways. For in that case the charge should not have been one of *contumacy* but of *divisiveness*. That however would have allowed those charged to raise a defence!

The January 2000 Commission – Division!

The charge of 'contumacy', as we have stated, is effectively impossible to defend. All that requires to be established is that the charge be found 'relevant.' In the Commission of January 2000 valiant efforts were made by the libelled men. These focussed strongly on the conviction that the Commission did not have the powers to act the way it was doing. The Principal Clerk (Professor John L. Mackay) felt the weight of this argument and advised the Commission to take it seriously. The Commission, however, ignored the advice and proceeded to find the libels relevant and serve them. This was somewhat of a formality when those accused confirmed that they held to their earlier resolve not to disband the FCDA. Administrative suspension followed immediately, though it must be said that the Commission was not *obliged* to serve the libels, as they did not at that point proceed to the 'proof' stage of the process. It is true that in the case of a 'contumacy' charge that would be a bit of a formality in any case.

---

[16] The description 'residuary Free Church' is not used in a derisory or disrespectful way. It is solely used to distinguish the part of the Free Church separate from the minority group which described itself as the *Free Church of Scotland (Continuing)*. 'Residuary' does not imply a 'smaller or lesser part' of a whole. (For example, the 'residuary' part of an estate may be very much larger than that part of an estate otherwise stipulated in a will.) There is a precedent for the use of this term in the early history of the Free Church. In the record of the General Assembly of the Free Church of Scotland in 1843 there is included "a sketch of the Proceedings of the Residuary Assembly." (Rev. John Baillie (Editor), *Proceedings of the General Assembly of the Free Church of Scotland; with a Sketch of the Proceedings of the Residuary Assembly*, Edinburgh, 1843).

The Commission, however, deferred the proof stage until the General Assembly in May. They clearly did not do that out of any concern for the libelled ministers, but simply to ensure in the interim that the members of the Commission would be duly protected in law (indemnified) in the event of their being found to have acted unlawfully in their decisions. In other words, the administrative suspensions appeared simply to be *tactical*, to ensure that the libelled men would be suspended from all the functions of the ministry, pending completion of the process in the May Assembly.

Given that they held firm convictions about the unlawfulness of the actions against them, the suspended men would not yield to what they considered to be wrongfully imposed upon them. Since there was effectively no defence against the contumacy charge, they would inevitably have been deposed in May, notwithstanding a complaint and appeal that had been lodged by dissenting brethren at the December Commission, when the decision had been taken to pursue libels upon those who did not disassociate from the FCDA. That would have required the matter to be raised in May, though it would hardly have made any difference given that in the meantime the suspended men would be out of their charges and unable to conduct their preaching and pastoral ministries or be appointed Commissioners to the General Assembly. That was a situation they were not prepared to accept. Therefore, those suspended on 20th January resolved to decline the authority of the Commission as then constituted and go elsewhere to resume the Commission and, as they saw it, continue the historic testimony of the Free Church. These men were then summarily suspended *sine die*.[17]

---

[17] A *sine die* suspension is one imposed without time limit normally 'for life,' apart, that is, from an appropriate expression of repentance for the fault considered to be proven. In terms of the Libels, deposition would almost certainly have resulted had the case gone to 'proof' (something of a formality in the case of contumacy). The case might have been considered as one of "aggravated contumacy" in which case the greater excommunication might also have been considered applicable. (See *Practice*, 193; and also pp191-196). Excommunication (greater or lesser) is not implicit in deposition, technically, but would inevitably have been involved in any sentence of deposition. As

Of those who were members of the Commission, five ministers signed a *Declinature*, stated in the following terms:

> We, the undersigned, protest against this Commission having reached a finding of relevancy in regard to Libels which are based on matters not condemned by the Word of God or the standards of the Church; and we further protest that, by this action, the Commission have disqualified themselves from being a duly constituted Commission of the General Assembly of this Church; wherefore we, in our name and in behalf of all who may adhere to us, hereby decline the jurisdiction of this Commission, declaring that we shall not be bound by any judgements pronounced in regard to us, and that we resolve to meet as a Commission of the General Assembly in a manner consonant with the constitution of the Church and with the Act of Assembly appointing this Commission. And the more effectually to carry out the said resolution, we call upon all members of this Commission who wish to remain loyal to the constitution of the Free Church of Scotland to assemble in Magdalen Chapel in the Cowgate of Edinburgh at 9.45pm to continue in a constitutional manner the present sederunt of the Commission.

This document was signed by 22 ministers in the Assembly Hall that evening of 20th January.[18] Since the Commission had already been constituted with the proper quorum (15), and since what was being done was a *continuation* of the same Commission, there was no inherent fault in this procedure. In this continuation of the Commission (as they saw it) they were joined by 17 other ministers who were present at the Commission. The 22 ministers, joined by elders and supportive people

stated elsewhere, it is a moot point whether the Commission, not being a Court of the Church, had powers to pass such sentences in any case. In the event the final 'sentence' of 20th January 2000, was in terms simply of suspension *sine die* and was silent on any other form of censure. (See *Acts and Proceedings of the General Assembly of the Free Church of Scotland*, Edinburgh 2000, 301).

[18] The ministers who signed the *Declinature* were: H M Ferrier, H J T Woods, A I M Maciver, D P Murray, D M MacDonald, G Craig, M MacLean, J MacLeod (Tarbat), A Murray, J I Gracie, J A Gillies, W Macleod, D N MacLeod, J Macleod (Duthil-Dores), H R M Radcliff, B H Baxter, J J Murray, J W Keddie, M A N Macleod, M J Roberts, J Morrison and K Macdonald. Of these, J MacLeod (Tarbat), J I Gracie, J A Gillies, W Macleod, and D N MacLeod were members of the Commission.

from throughout the Church, re-gathered at the Magdalen Chapel in the Cowgate that evening and continued, as they saw it, the Commission of Assembly, approving a *Declaration of Reconstitution*.[19] This was signed by 19 ministers and 18 elders that evening.[20]

The *Declaration* was and is an historical document expository of the claims of the Free Church of Scotland (Continuing) to continuity with the historic position of the Free Church of Scotland. It was and is explanatory of the events that had led to the formation of a continuing Free Church, claiming complete continuity with the Disruption Church, and with the remnant that continued the Free Church testimony after the union of 1900. No doubt the protesting brethren were not beyond criticism in some of the ways issues were addressed. Their concern, however, was conscientiously for truth and righteousness, and historical continuity.

These documents form the basis of the claim of the minority that it was not a 'secession', whatever may have been maintained either by the residuary Free Church or for that matter the decisions of subsequent law cases. There was a sad division, but the responsibility for that division is another matter in determining claims to being heirs of the Free Church, notwithstanding any subsequent failure on the part of one or the other at civil law to sustain these claims. The failure to apply the *Form of Process* properly and the evident abuse of the powers

---

[19] The text of the *Declaration of Reconstitution* adopted that same evening is provided in full in Appendix 2. The *Declaration* provides an explicit record of the claims of what has become known as the 'Free Church of Scotland (Continuing)'. For a contemporary reflection on the events surrounding the Division of 2000 see the booklet *The Division of 2000. Some Questions and Answers on the Division in the Free Church of Scotland 20th January 2000* (Published by the Free Church of Scotland (Continuing), January 2001).

[20] See Appendix 1 for all the ministers and elders who adhered to the Free Church of Scotland (Continuing) on the evening of 20th January 2000 (together with the names of ministers who subsequently adhered to the Church). The name 'Free Church of Scotland (Continuing)' was adopted for *administrative purposes*, as the men who maintained that they were continuing the Commission that night did not claim to be anything other than the Free Church of Scotland. The ministers who signed the *Declinature* in the Assembly Hall that evening are separately indicated (†) in Appendix 1. (No elders' names were attached to the *Declinature*).

of Commissions of Assembly were critical concerns in justifying, in the view of the dissenting group, the *Declinature* and *Declaration* of 2000 and the just claim to be a continuing Free Church of Scotland.

The Free Church of Scotland (Continuing) emerges

Those who were party to the reconstitution of the Commission of Assembly on 20th January 2000 made a clear claim to continuity with the historic Free Church. An implication of this was that they denied that they had taken part in a secession. They adopted the term 'Continuing' simply for administrative purposes. They were under no illusion that the brethren from whom they were now separate would consider them and wish them to be considered *seceders*. That was not a position the 'Continuing' men would accept. They had no desire to separate from the Free Church, and were it not for what they considered unlawful, shameful and oppressive misapplication of disciplinary process that, they believed, violated important aspects of the Church's constitution, they would not be separate.

The reason for the separation was not, however, merely *administrative*. It was not simply because of a misapplication of proper Church procedures that there was a division in the Church. The men who formed the Free Church of Scotland (Continuing) did not consider themselves to be guilty of *schism*. To the contrary they maintained that important constitutional principles had been violated by the majority, especially in three particulars:

(1) *Actions of the majority involved a violation of the integrity of the ministerial ordination vows.* The finding of October 1999, with reference to the FCDA involved an implicit alteration to ordination vows to make the FCDA unlawful and attachment to it at odds with being a Free Church minister or elder. It was an imposition of a prohibition not specified in the Questions or Formula, and not justified (the FCDA men believed) as a censurable offence. The libelled men held that such a declaration amounted to arbitrary law and that it was therefore a violation of the contract between the minister and the

Church and undermined the integrity of the ordination vows. The minister has a responsibility to be faithful to his vows. By the same token, the Church has a responsibility towards its ministers not to impose upon them what is not explicitly disallowed in the constitution of the Church. The crux of course lies in the justification for declaring the FCDA *qua* FCDA as following a 'divisive course', and in turn assuming that that would be inclusive of all members of the FCDA individually. However, there was no 'case' involving the FCDA (obviously) nor was there care about adopting such an *ad hoc* 'declaratory' Act without recognising an impact it could have on ordination vows.

(2) *Actions of the majority involved a violation of the principle of the Headship of Christ.* Christ is the Head of the Church. The Church is subject to Him and His Word and may go no farther than His Word allows. In this case the libelled and suspended men held that by imposing upon them charges not demonstrably contrary to the Word of God the majority was assuming an arbitrary and authoritarian (or *magisterial*) position, and in that particular concern they were acting inconsistently with the principle of Christ's headship in the Church. The declaring of ministers to be guilty of sin and denying their ordination vows in virtue of being part of the Free Church Defence Association may be considered to be an implicit denial of the headship of Christ. The Church is to act *ministerially* under Christ and is under obligation not to impose rules or processes which are not grounded in His Word or the Church's constitution.[21]

(3) *Actions of the majority involved implicit or constructive denials of the right to exercise protest, and right to continue in protest, against findings or decisions of the Church which were conscientiously considered to be at odds with a right view*

---

[21] Cf.: "Although the General Assembly is invested with the power of regulating the whole action of the Church in its Synods, Presbyteries and Kirk Sessions, still it is not regarded as having any lordly or absolutely binding authority. It is expected to act ministerially under Christ, and to carry out such rules as appear to harmonise with His own instructions in His Word" (*The Practice of the Free Church of Scotland*, Edinburgh, [8]1995, 82).

of the doctrine, worship, practice or government of the Church in any respect.
The FCDA and those who supported it considered that the
concerns raised in its magazine were perfectly consistent with the
constitutional position of the Church and the ordination vows. It
was further considered to be within the rights of those who raised
these concerns to continue to protest about failures to address them
adequately and biblically. Indeed, they felt it was their constitutional
duty to do so in the interests solely of truth and righteousness,
however uncomfortable it made themselves or others feel. In this
respect it was felt that the implicit 'gagging orders' in relation to the
1995 finding in the matter of allegations against the Professor, and
in relation to the October 1999, finding regarding the FCDA, were
unconstitutional and effective denials of a right to exercise protest
involving an intention to continue to do so until *right* is seen to be
established in the Church. In contentious or disputed issues, unless
the matters protested about are demonstrated on good grounds to
be groundless or ill-conceived, or are adequately and effectively
addressed, continuing protest cannot be denied.

On the question of *continuing protest*, in the June Commission of
Assembly in 1999 the then Principal Clerk (Rev. Professor John L.
Mackay) is reported as stating that once a protest was lodged an
individual had no right to continue raising the matter: "The only
honourable course of action was to leave [the Church], if the individual
felt so aggrieved as to be unable to remain silent on the issue."[22] In the
history of the Free Church, however, there was a well-established
tradition from the 19th century of men continuing to speak out on
issues about which they had protested.[23] The fact is that the Church had
never endorsed the Principal Clerk's position. Protest is among a range
of expressions of dissent, the exercise of which was always recognised
as a right of office-bearers. In addition, protesters were always

---

[22] *The Monthly Record*, August 1999, 180.
[23] For example, on issues of Union negotiations in the late 1860s and later in the
century, as well as various concerns in relation and the use of uninspired materials for
praise and instrumental music in public worship, and to the Declaratory Act of 1892.

recognised as *maintaining* their protests on matters arising on any such issues later and as being perfectly free to seek to correct perceived wrongs. It would be a grievous injustice to consider such individuals as following a 'divisive course' or as being made to feel that they must leave the church, however uncomfortable it may be for some in the church.[24]

In 1999 the Assembly and Commissions issued a number of instructions to members and office bearers of the Church which were protested against. What then was the duty of those who protested these instructions? The issue, however, will turn on the question: Were the instructions *lawful?* In this controversy, not only was the instruction of the Moderator to Mr Roberts at the May Assembly (1999) of dubious lawfulness, to say the least, the subsequent finding with reference to the status of the 1995 decision on the matter of allegations against a Professor was also questionable, to say the least. In the former, the instruction was given based on a statement which remained unexplained. In relation to the 1995 finding, office-bearers and members were required not to pursue matters dealt with in that finding *in any form whatsoever.* This meant that the Commission in June 1999 ruled, *inter alia*, that it was unlawful for anyone in the Church, subsequently, to repeat a statement in the *Report* of the Special Commission (1999) that the 1995 finding was 'unsafe.' Was this instruction lawful or unlawful? Was the 1995 finding a *safe* finding or was it not? Those who maintained that these instructions were not lawful could not be expected to renege on their protests, nor their free association with the FCDA for that matter. Furthermore, to have left the Church, as they saw it, would have involved them in schism. As indicated above, the June 1999 Commission decision on the 1995

---

[24] It is a different thing if what a person maintained is *demonstrably* at variance with the doctrine or practice of the Church. In that case he would rightly be disciplined, but not for simply continuing conscientiously to hold in a disputed matter to a 'protest', such as the issue that perplexed the Church throughout the 1990s, albeit under the guise of 'contumacy,' or a questionably 'lawful' finding.

finding can itself be seen as involving an imposition on ordination vows.

Fallout from the Division

The situations in the congregations of the ministers and elders supportive of the dissenting position varied widely. In some instances entire congregations, more or less, were behind their minister and dissenting elders. In other cases there was barely majority support and in several instances there was minority support. After the result of the Commission on January 20th and the 'reconstitution' at the Magdalen Chapel, there were in many cases stressful tensions in local situations. A sad feature of such disputes is the separation of brethren, even within families. Clearly a serious issue related to the occupation of properties. At that point there was a 'face-off' between the fractured parts of the Free Church. As a minority, those who adhered to the *Declaration of Reconstitution* did not see themselves as schismatic. They therefore did not concede that they had no rightful claim, in whole or in part, to properties occupied. Obviously, this was a contentious issue and strongly disputed, especially since the Free Church major part in the division laid claim to all properties and funds. In some cases ministers and people supporting the 'continuing' Church walked away from properties and other arrangements were made. In some cases churches and manses were eventually built or purchased. In the end there was no Church-wide agreement reached and, sadly, legal action was pursued. However, subsequently there were some amicable settlements over the transfer of congregational properties to Free Church of Scotland (Continuing) congregations.[25]

---

[25] It was reported to the General Assembly of the Free Church of Scotland (Continuing) in 2017 that the total purchase value of Church and manse buildings owned by congregations at the end of 2016 amounted to some £4.5m.

WHERE TO NOW?

It is sad that the history of the Free Church of Scotland in the 20th century should culminate in a division at the beginning of the last year of the millennium. Not least was this unwelcome because it caused a split in the largest constitutional confessional Church remaining in Scotland. Since 2000 the smaller section of that division – Free Church of Scotland (Continuing) – comprising only about 15% of the whole[1] – has faced considerable difficulties and very limited resources in seeking faithfully to maintain its continuing commitment to the Headship of Christ and the Confessional, Calvinistic constitutional position of the historic Free Church in Scotland.

Following on from the division, to clarify matters at law, the Free Church of Scotland (Continuing), repudiating the notion that it was a secession, took out a case at law against the Free Church of Scotland in the Court of Session. The case for litigation sought to aver that continuing to protest on disputed issues was a right constructively denied by the majority in the Church courts in 1999/2000. In the event the case was not successful before Lady Paton in the Court of Session. She recognised that there was a right of protest that had been exercised in the Free Church historically but did not see this as a fundamental principal of the Free Church. In 2005 she found in favour of the majority, although she did state that the smaller group – the Free Church of Scotland (Continuing) – had itself not departed from any fundamental principle of the historic Free Church. The Assembly agreed to appeal against Lady Paton's finding but as the necessary funds were not available and the Church was unwilling to place individual members under liability, the Church ultimately fell from its appeal. It should be noted that Lady Paton's judgement is an opinion, not law.[2]

---

[1] As indicated in Appendix 1, 21% of the total ministry of the Church at the time adhered to the Free Church of Scotland (Continuing) at and after January 2000.

In 2007 the Free Church (residuary) took an action in the Court of Session in relation to the properties at Broadford on the Isle of Skye. In this case the Court of Session in the Outer House (2009) and later, after appeal, in the Inner House (2011), ruled that the Free Church of Scotland (Continuing) had left the Free Church of Scotland and was therefore not entitled to any of the assets of the Free Church. It should be noted, however, that this judgement did not rule on any fundamental principles of the Free Church.[3]

Notwithstanding the outcome of these court cases the Free Church of Scotland (Continuing) still claims "to be the true *bona fide* representatives of the original protesters of 1843 and to be carrying out the objects of the Protest more faithfully than the majority."[4] This claim has effectively been strengthened by the movement in the larger body away from the time-honoured post-1900 Free Church principles of worship by their decision in a plenary Assembly of November 2010. In that plenary Assembly the post-1900 Acts in the Free Church maintaining the exclusive use of inspired materials of praise, unaccompanied, in public worship, were repealed.[5]

Another Free Church continuing

At the time of writing [2017] the Church has 45 ministers, including 18 retired men, and 2 probationers. It comprises 36 congregations or preaching stations including several congregations overseas. It has an interest in missionary work in Zambia, Sri Lanka, and Spain, and a Seminary (partly distance learning) to train men for the ministry, with 5

---

[2] For the details of this opinion see *Free Church of Scotland (Continuing) v General Assembly of the Free Church of Scotland* [2005] Court of Session Outer House 46, 2005 SC396.

[3] For the details of these cases see *Smith, Moderator of the General Assembly of the Free Church of Scotland, et al. v Morrison, et al.* [2009] Court of Session Outer House 113; [2011] Court of Session Inner House 52.

[4] See *Declaration of Reconstitution*, in Appendix 2, page 102.

[5] *Acts of the Plenary General Assembly of November, 2010*. Act 1 – Act anent Public Worship (No. 1 of Class II).
(See, http://freechurch.org/assets/documents/2014/Acts_of_Assembly2011.pdf. Accessed 5 October 2016).

lecturers, based in Inverness, with Home Mission work in Scotland and a widely respected Church Magazine (*Free Church Witness*).

The doctrinal commitment of the Free Church of Scotland (Continuing) is precisely what had been confessed historically by the Free Church, as reaffirmed after 1900. It holds unequivocally to the whole doctrine contained in the *Confession of Faith* as its subordinate standard and to the doctrine, worship, government and discipline of the Scottish Reformed Church, particularly as expressed in the historical standards of the Free Church of Scotland.[6] It maintains the practice of purity of worship, believing that only unaccompanied inspired materials of praise have Scripture warrant for use in public worship. It affirms the doctrines of grace commonly known as Calvinism, summed up in the 'five points': total depravity, unconditional election, limited atonement, irresistible grace, and perseverance of the saints.[7] As a gospel church it is 'evangelical' in maintaining the free gospel call to repent and believe in Christ, and responsibility for evangelism in terms of the Great Commission of the Lord Jesus Christ (Matthew 28:19, 20). Presbyterian in Church government, with the Disruption Church (1843) the Free Church of Scotland (Continuing) holds to the Headship of Christ in Church and State, involving the responsibility of the State to maintain Christian faith but not so that the spiritual independence of the Church is infringed.

As with any Church claiming to be evangelical and reformed, for all its limited resources, its strength will be found in faithfulness to the Lord Jesus Christ, the King of kings, the Lord of lords, the Head of the Church and the Head of nations (1 Timothy 6:15-16; Ephesians 1:19-23), and perseverance in that faithfulness (James 1:12). What future and role do the Free Church or Free Church of Scotland

---

[6] See the *Subordinate Standards and Other Authoritative Documents of the Free Church of Scotland*, particularly the editions produced with the 'Act and Declaration anent the Publication of the Subordinate Standards, and Other Authoritative Documents of the Free Church of Scotland' of 31st May 1851.

[7] See John W Keddie, *The Five Points of Calvinism*, Free Church of Scotland (Continuing), 2010, for a concise outline of this teaching.

(Continuing) have? In faithfulness to Him there is a future and a hope (Jeremiah 29:11).

Though a radical change was made in its worship forms in 2010, the Free Church of Scotland, the larger section of the division of 2000, still also formally maintains adherence to the *Westminster Confession of Faith* as its principal subordinate standard. It is ostensibly a confessional Reformed Church claiming direct lineage with the Church of the Scottish Reformation and of the Disruption Church of 1843. In addition, it continues to maintain active mission and outreach work at home and overseas and also operates a fully-staffed College with some of its divinity courses validated by the University of Glasgow.[8] The College was officially (re-)launched as *Edinburgh Theological Seminary* from 21st May 2014.

The ready acceptance of different worship forms repudiated by the post-1900 Free Church, and an evidently broader understanding of the implications of ordination vows raises questions about the commitment of the Free Church (residuary) to a whole-hearted affirmation of Reformed faith and worship. Since 2000 the Free Church has admitted numerous ministers, elders and people from the Church of Scotland in the wake of the acceptance by that Church of openly homosexual and lesbian ministers. What impact this will have on the Free Church remains to be seen. The Free Church (residuary) clearly has shown a vision for a national evangelical church. To what extent this is being pursued with a consequent dilution of a strictly Reformed outlook and practice is a real question. Time will tell. One thing is evident, it has drifted from the position of the men who maintained the Free Church witness through the turbulent events at the time of the Union of 1900 and the years that followed.

---

[8] Initially (1999) it was expected that the University of Edinburgh would validate a B.Th. degree (*Principal Acts of the General Assembly of the Free Church of Scotland*, Act XXIII – Act anent Validation of B.Th. Degree (No. 23 of Class II) Edinburgh, 13th May 1999). In the event validation was to come through the University of Glasgow (B.Th., 2002; M.Th., 2005).

'Minorities' not to be despised

It is recognized that there is no virtue in being a 'minority,' in and of itself. Great care has to be taken not to be pretentious or self-righteous. There is no perfect Church on earth, and there is certainly no virtue in censoriousness or carnal pride. Nevertheless, a minority may continue to hold something precious that may be in danger of being lost from the Church-life of a nation. This, at any rate, is the conviction of the Free Church of Scotland (Continuing). Not that it considers itself better than others. It simply has sought with a good conscience to hold firm to the Scottish Reformation and Disruption heritage. The issue of its survival lies with the Head of the Church.

Where to now?

Relations between the two splintered parts of the Free Church for the greater part remained tense with little prospect of a rapprochement between the two parts. Without recognition on the part of the residuary Free Church of violations of principle involved in the contentious decisions of Commissions of 1999 and January 2000 leading to the division of 2000 the coming together of the splintered parts of the Free Church is not easy to envisage. By an Act of a Commission of Assembly held in December 2008, the Free Church purported to terminate the sentences of suspension on all the ministers subsequently associated with the Free Church of Scotland (Continuing). This was done "solely" (it was stated) based on recognising the Free Church of Scotland (Continuing) as a denomination, albeit *without any formal communication of the finding being intimated to the suspended ministers*!

Thus, the formerly suspended ministers were regarded as ministers in good standing in a Christian Church. This was done consciously *without any requirement of an expression of repentance*. The claim was made that this "ought not to be interpreted as a departure by the Free Church of Scotland from the principle that evidence of repentance is due from parties under discipline prior to their being restored."[9] By

---

[9] Acts of Commission of Assembly, Act VI – *Act terminating sentence of Suspension on former*

any measure, however, it was an arbitrary enactment, given the fact that
the men in question had received a *sine die* suspension and had not
repented their perceived fault. But if the initial discipline applied was
considered righteous, for the honour of God, for the good of the
Church and in the cause of truth, then such a 'termination' without due
repentance/correction must be either unrighteous or an admission of
the inappropriateness of the discipline originally exercised. It gave the
impression of the exercise of mercy over judgement. That, however,
would only have been credible within the context of repentance for
faults apparently so grievous as to lead to *sine die* suspension. It was in
effect a hollow 'sleight on hand' in Church discipline. As such it was
designed to help the Free Church rather than the suspended ministers,
in that they could enter into dealings with them over properties, funds
and church records as well as no doubt make them appear
magnanimous in the eyes of other Churches. Any rapprochement
between the Churches, however, has been made more unlikely by the
abandonment of the 'purity of worship' principle on the part of the
residuary Free Church in November 2010, as referred to above.

Whatever anyone – whether ecclesiastical or civil courts – thinks
of the so-called 'continuing' Church and what it is, the 'reconstituted'
body claims identity with the Disruption Church and the continuing
Free Church of 1900. This claim continues to be part of its clear
testimony and a *de facto* element in its committed position. At any rate,
the Free Church of Scotland (Continuing) still stands directly in the line
of the principles and practices espoused by the Free Church fathers of
the immediate post-1900 period, notwithstanding adverse judgements
in civil courts. This claim has additional weight in the light of changes
in the Free Church subsequently to 2000, especially in the area of purity
of worship. As stated in a declaration by the Free Church of Scotland
(Continuing) General Assembly of May, 2014[10]: "The General

Ministers, Edinburgh, 3rd December 2008.
[10] *The Principal Acts of the General Assembly of the Free Church of Scotland (Continuing)*, Act
XVII – Act anent Legislation Prior to 20th January, 2000, Edinburgh, 22nd May, 2014.

Assembly reaffirm that they are the true *bona fide* successor of the Free Church of Scotland of 1843; and; The General Assembly hereby declare that legislation enacted by the Free Church of Scotland prior to 20th January, 2000 applies to the Free Church of Scotland (Continuing) in the same way as any legislation enacted by the said Free Church of Scotland (Continuing) after 20th January 2000."

APPENDIX 1

FREE CHURCH MINISTERS AND ELDERS WHO ADHERED TO THE FREE CHURCH OF SCOTLAND (CONTINUING) AT AND AFTER 2000

(1) Ministers who signed the *Declaration of Reconstitution* on 20th January 2000

Bryan H. Baxter, rtd., Kilwinning & Saltcoats (Ord., 1965) †

Graeme Craig, Lochalsh & Glenshiel (Ord., 1989) †

Hugh M. Ferrier, rtd., Free North, Inverness (Ord., 1952) †

John A. Gillies, rtd., Partick Highland, Glasgow (Ord., 1961) †

James I. Gracie, North Uist & Grimsay (Ord., 1994) †

John W. Keddie, Bracadale, Isle of Skye (Ord., 1987) †

Donald M. MacDonald, rtd., Uig, Isle of Lewis (Ord., 1976) †

Kenneth Macdonald, Snizort, Isle of Skye (Ord., 1997) †

Allan I. M. MacIver, Strath, Isle of Skye (Ord., 1964) †

Malcolm MacLean, rtd., North Tolsta, Isle of Lewis (Ord., 1965) †

Donald N. MacLeod, rtd, Briton Street, Glasgow (Ord., 1972) †

John MacLeod, Tarbat (Ord., 1978) †

John Macleod, Duthil-Dores (Ord., 1983) †

William Macleod, Portree, Isle of Skye (Ord., 1976) †

John Morrison, Kilmuir & Stenscholl, Isle of Skye (Ord., 1975) †

Allan Murray, Rogart & Eddrachillis (Ord., 1988) †

David P. Murray, Lochcarron (Ord., 1995) †

John J. Murray, Free St. Columba's, Edinburgh (Ord., 1978) †

Henry J. T. Woods, Paisley (Ord., 1982) †

[19]

96   A Divided Church

(2) Ministers ordained in the Free Church who adhered to the Free Church of Scotland (Continuing) after 20ᵗʰ January, 2000:

David Compton, rtd., Toronto (Ord., 1970)

David S. Fraser, South African Mission Field (Ord., 1970)

James Frew, Kiltearn (Ord., 1997)

John J. Harding, Shettleston (Ord., 1979)

Alasdair Johnston, rtd., Dumbarton (Ord., 1950)

Robert W. Josey, rtd., Resolis (Ord., 1971)

Ronald Mackenzie, rtd., Glenelg and Arnisdale (Ord., 1976)

Daniel Mackinnon, rtd., Kilmorack and Strathglass (Ord. 1980)

Murdo A. N. Macleod, Leverburgh, Harris (Ord., 1995) †

Murdo Macaulay MacLeod, rtd., Barvas, Isle of Lewis (Ord., 1967)

Roderick Macleod, rtd., Dundee (Ord., 1966)

Innes Macrae, rtd., Tain (Ord., 1983)(Died 25ᵗʰ March, 2000)*

William McKnight, rtd, Leith (Ord. in Baptist Church, 1971; Adm., 1980)

H. R. Moshe Radcliff, minister without charge (Ord. in Church of England, 1960; Adm., 1988) †

Maurice J. Roberts, Greyfriars, Inverness (Ord., 1974) †

William B. Scott, Dumfries (Ord., 1972)

Iain Smith, Partick, Glasgow (Ord., 1994)

Kenneth Smith, rtd., Knock, Isle of Lewis (Ord.1968)

[18]

† Ministers who signed the *Declinature* in the Assembly Hall [22]
* Action was not taken against Innes Macrae for health reasons, though he unquestionably affiliated himself to the minority.

[20 ministers in charges plus 17 retired ministers = 37]
[37÷173=21.4%= dissenting ministers as a percentage of the Free Church ministry at the end of 1999]

Note regarding background of ministers:

(1) *Length of service:*

It will be seen that most of the ministers adhering to the dissenting group had been ordained in the 1970s and earlier. The 'alignment' of the FCC showed that 62% of them had been ordained prior to 1980.

Ordained in the 1950s	2	(5%)
Ordained in the 1960s	7	(19%)
Ordained in the 1970s	14	(38%)
Ordained in the 1980s	7	(19%)
Ordained in the 1990s	7	(19%)
	37	

In other words, this was not a group of immature or inexperienced servants of the Free Church.

(2) *Regional background:*

In terms of regional background, the majority of the FCC ministers were from the Highlands and Islands. The breakdown was representative of the ministry as a whole:

Highlands and Islands	25 (68%)
Lowlands	6 (16%)
English/Overseas	6 (16%)
	37

In other words, this was decidedly not a group predominantly comprised of lowland or English 'entryists.'

(3) Elders who signed the *Declaration of Reconstitution* on 20th January 2000

John Bain (Snizort, Isle of Skye)

Harley J. Cameron (Glasgow, St Vincent Street)

Norman Campbell (Edinburgh, St Columba's)

Maurice Grant (Edinburgh, St Columba's)

Peter K. MacAskill (Strath, Isle of Skye)

Roderick MacKay (Snizort, Isle of Skye)

Donald A. MacKenzie (East Kilbride)

John MacKenzie (Assynt)

John A. MacLeod (Snizort, Isle of Skye)

John A. Macpherson (Glasgow, Briton Street)

John MacPherson (Portree, Isle of Skye)

Peter B. Matheson (Duirinish, Isle of Skye)

Alasdair Morrison (Lochalsh & Glenshiel)

Alexander Morrison (Edinburgh, St Columba's)

D. William Munro (Lairg)

Murdoch Murchison (Strathpeffer, Strathconon & Garve)

Alasdair N. Nicolson (Bracadale, Isle of Skye)

Angus Shaw (Snizort, Isle of Skye)

[18]

Note:
Besides the ministers adhering to the continuing Free Church in 2000 there were around 140 office-bearers, 100 ruling elders and 40 deacons.

APPENDIX 2

DECLARATION OF RECONSTITUTION (2000)[1]

*(Signed by 19 ministers and 18 elders in the Magdalen Chapel,
Edinburgh on 20th January 2000)*

We the undersigned Ministers and Elders of the Free Church of Scotland,
Considering that the constitution of the said Church is contained in the
Scriptures of the Old and New Testaments, the Westminster Confession of
Faith as approved by the General Assembly of the Church of Scotland in 1647,
the First and Second Books of Discipline, the Larger and Shorter Catechisms,
the Claim, Declaration, and Protest of 1842, the Protest of 1843, the Act of
Separation and Deed of Demission executed in 1843, the Formula appointed
to be subscribed by probationers before receiving licence and by all office-
bearers at the time of their admission together with the Questions appointed to
be put to the said parties at ordination and admission, and the Acts of
Assembly of the Church of Scotland prior to 1843; and now seeing:

(1st) That Commissioners exercising a majority in voting in the General
Assemblies and Commissions of the Free Church of Scotland, and purporting
to enact and make findings in the name of the Free Church of Scotland and by
authority as office-bearers according to the rule of Christ and the constitution
of the Church, have of late years applied in an arbitrary and tyrannical way the
resolutions of its General Assemblies and Commissions, establishing these as
ultimate rules of conduct, and treating as contumacious any conscientious
inability to give obedience to edicts of the said Assemblies and Commissions,
contrary to Chapter XXXI Section IV of the Confession of Faith, which states:
"All Synods or Councils since the Apostles' times, whether general or
particular, may err, and many have erred; therefore they are not to be made the
rule of faith or practice, but to be used as an help in both"; and Chapter XX

---

[1] In order to clarify its position in relation to the claims made in the 'Declaration' and
the subsequent decisions of law cases bearing on such claims, the Free Church of
Scotland (Continuing) at its Assembly of 2014 declared: "(1) The General Assembly
reaffirm that they are the true *bona fide* successor of the Free Church of Scotland of
1843; and; (2) The General Assembly hereby declare that legislation enacted by the Free
Church of Scotland prior to 20th January, 2000 applies to the Free Church of Scotland
(Continuing) in the same way as any legislation enacted by the said Free Church of
Scotland (Continuing) after 20th January 2000."

Section II which states: "God alone is Lord of the conscience, and hath left it free from the doctrines and commandments of men which are in anything contrary to his Word, or beside it, in matters of faith or worship, so that to believe such doctrines, or to obey such commandments out of conscience, is to betray true liberty of conscience; and the requiring of an implicit faith, and an absolute and blind obedience, is to destroy liberty of conscience, and reason also": by, *inter alia*:

(a) deeming it censurable to refuse to obey instructions of a Church Court which are in violation of the Word of God and the constitution of the Free Church of Scotland, regardless of whether obedience could be rendered in conscience or not;

(b) bringing disciplinary processes against ministers and elders in respect of matters which have not been declared censurable in Scripture;

(c) treating as potentially contumacious any suggestion to revisit an administrative decision of the General Assembly notwithstanding that such decisions are not unalterable and are open at all times to review, and instituting disciplinary processes against ministers who called for such review;

(d) appointing general assessors to a Presbytery in order to impose the will of the General Assembly and its Commission on the will of the substantial majority of the Presbytery conscientiously expressed;

(e) declaring sinfully schismatic, without proof before the Courts of the Church, the action of a body of believers who withdrew from their local congregation for conscience' sake and out of concern for the correct observance of the constitution of the Free Church of Scotland, and forbidding ministers and office-bearers, under pain of censure, to preach to or have fellowship with the said body of believers notwithstanding that they have not departed from the constitution and principles of the Church;

(2nd) That commissioners purporting to exercise lawful judicial authority in the name of the Free Church of Scotland have breached fundamental principles of equity and natural justice, contrary to Chapter XIX, Section V of the Confession of Faith, which states: "The moral law doth for ever bind all, as well justified persons as others, to the obedience thereof; and that not only in the matter contained in it, but also in respect of the authority of God the Creator, who gave it; neither doth Christ in the gospel anyway dissolve, but much strengthen this obligation": by, *inter alia*:

(a) forbidding office-bearers and members now or henceforth to pursue matters arising from a particular *fama*, involving serious allegations against a minister, in any form whatsoever;

(b) ordering the destruction of documents relating to the aforesaid *fama* notwithstanding that issues arising therefrom remain unresolved, thereby prejudicing the rights of interested parties to secure a fair and proper resolution of the said issues;

(c) imposing requirements on ministers and office-bearers additional to their ordination vows, and thereby, in particular, infringing their civil rights to freedom of assembly and association by forbidding them, under pain of censure, to hold office in an association professedly aiming to assert and defend the constitution of the historic Free Church of Scotland;

(d) annulling the licensing of, and withdrawing recognition as a candidate for the ministry from, a divinity student who had been accepted by the Training of the Ministry and Admissions Committee after due examination of his credentials and then licensed by his Presbytery in accordance with the law of the Church, and against whom no disciplinary proceedings had been brought, and directing the Presbytery to expunge the decision to proceed to license from its minutes;

(3rd) That albeit the Form of Process enacted by the General Assembly of the Church of Scotland in 1707, and being a constitutional document of the Free Church of Scotland, is binding and obligatory on all Courts of the said Church, Commissioners purporting to exercise lawful judicial authority in the name of the Free Church of Scotland have adopted findings and conducted procedures at variance with, and subversive of, the principles of church discipline set out in the said Form of Process and reflected in the authorised practice and procedure of the Free Church of Scotland, by, inter alia:

(a) endorsing a finding of the Training of the Ministry and Admissions Committee, in relation to the aforesaid *fama*, without judicial examination of the evidence and without enquiry to ensure that the precognition in the case had been properly conducted and that all relevant witnesses had been duly examined, contrary to the requirement of the Form of Process that when such a matter comes before a church judicatory it ought not to be "negligently inquired into" (Chapter VII, paragraph 2);

(b) treating the said decision as judicial notwithstanding that the procedure adopted by the judicatory was not conducted under the Form of Process and the decision was therefore no more than administrative;

(c) purporting to terminate the bringing of private libels in relation to the aforesaid *fama*, thereby seeking to prohibit a course of action to which the Form of Process (Chapter VII, paragraph 3) gives a right;

(d) conducting disciplinary processes against ministers before the Commission of Assembly as a court of first instance, in violation of the requirement in the Form of Process (Chapter VII, paragraph 1) that all processes against any minister are to begin before his Presbytery, and using the said Commission to institute such processes without authority from the General Assembly:

And that Commissioners exercising a majority in voting in the General

Assemblies and Commissions of Assemblies, purporting to act lawfully therein
in the name of the Free Church of Scotland, have, by the aforementioned
actions, passed acts and resolutions under which the constitution and
standards of the Free Church of Scotland can be, and are violated, and have
refused to countenance petitions and other requests for redress of the same;
whereby the said persons have ceased to constitute authoritative courts of the
historic Free Church of Scotland.

In consequence whereof, –
We claim our right and profess our duty, according to our ordination vows
thereanent, to administer discipline and government consistent with the
requirements embodied in the constitution of the Free Church of Scotland and
stated in our ordination vows, which vows bind us to maintain the said
discipline and government "notwithstanding of whatsoever trouble or
persecution may arise";
We protest that by our engagement to the constitution of the Free Church of
Scotland, our office in the said Church prevents, and has always prevented, our
being bound by any acts or resolutions (including, but not confined to, the
foregoing) of the said persons purporting to act lawfully in the name of the
Free Church of Scotland, which are contrary to the authorised standards of the
Free Church of Scotland;
We declare that in accordance with the Word of God and the authorised
standards of the Free Church of Scotland, we are not and can never be under
the jurisdiction of individuals and courts purporting to act in the name of the
Free Church of Scotland, yet against the said Word and standards, without
doing violence to our consciences and our faithfulness to our ordination vows.

Wherefore, –
We have resolved to declare that the Free Church of Scotland is separate from
all church courts seeking to impose acts and findings contrary to the
constitution of the historic Free Church of Scotland, and we claim still to be
the true *bona fide* representatives of the original protesters of 1843 and to be
carrying out the objects of the Protest more faithfully than the majority.
In order the more formally and effectually to carry out the said resolution, we,
the Ministers and Elders of the historic Free Church of Scotland under-
subscribing, for ourselves and all who may now or hereafter adhere to us,
affirming that we and they now adhere as we and they have heretofore done to
the constitution and standards of the historic Free Church of Scotland, declare
that we hereby disassociate ourselves from any residual subsisting body
claiming the title of the Free Church of Scotland; and we further specially
provide and declare:
That we for ourselves, and all who may now or hereafter adhere to us, in no
degree abandon, impair or waive the rights belonging to us as ministers of

Christ's gospel, and pastors and elders of particular congregations, to perform fully and freely the functions of our offices towards our respective congregations, or such portions thereof as may adhere to us;

That signature of or adherence to this Declaration shall in no way prejudice our right to maintain the doctrines and principles of the historic Free Church of Scotland as set forth in her authorised standards and authoritative documents and to take all steps that may be necessary to vindicate the said doctrines and principles;

That we are and shall be free to exercise government and discipline in our several judicatories according to the Word of God and consistent with the constitution and standards of the historic Free Church of Scotland;

That henceforth we are not and shall not be subject in any respect to the ecclesiastical judicatories of any residual subsisting body claiming the title of the Free Church of Scotland;

That meanwhile, to distinguish the reconstituted Free Church of Scotland (solely for purposes of administration) from any residual body claiming that title we may be called the Free Church of Scotland (Continuing);

That the rights and benefits accruing to the ministers subscribing, or who may hereafter adhere hereto, from the pension and other funds of the Free Church of Scotland are hereby reserved;

That this Declaration shall in no way be held as a renunciation on the part of the said ministers of their rights to the ownership, enjoyment and occupation of the property and funds of the Free Church of Scotland, including but not limited to churches, manses, halls and other heritable properties, nor of any rights which may be found to belong to such ministers or to their congregations or to the office bearers of such congregations or to existing or future trustees on behalf of such congregations or their kirk-sessions in regard to the same;

That there is hereby reserved to us, the subscribers hereto, and to all who may now or hereafter adhere to us, power and authority to take all steps that may be necessary or expedient to declare, vindicate, enforce and preserve the status, rights and privileges of every kind, both ecclesiastical and civil, of and attaching now and in the future to us and all who may now or hereafter adhere to us, as those remaining faithful to the doctrine, government and principles embodied in the supreme and subordinate standards of the historic Free Church of Scotland.

The subscribers call to witness the Christian people of this land, and of the Reformed fellowship throughout the world, that this action is not lightly entered into. It is taken in sorrow at the enforced parting from brethren with whom we have had fellowship in the Lord, but also in defence of truth and justice and of the historic principles and practice of the Free Church of Scotland.

We declare that if any residual body continuing to claim the title of the Free Church of Scotland is prepared to return to the constitution and standards of the historic Free Church of Scotland, and to practise and adhere faithfully to the same, we will see it as our duty to seek reconciliation with our brethren within that body.